New Bern

New Bern

Tales from the Inner Banks

Bill Hand

The History Press

Published by The History Press
Charleston, SC 29403
www.historypress.net

First published 2011

Manufactured in the United States

ISBN 978.1.60949.373.8

Library of Congress Cataloging-in-Publication Data

Hand, Bill, 1956-
New Bern : tales from the inner banks / Bill Hand.
p. cm.
Includes bibliographical references.
ISBN 978-1-60949-373-8
1. New Bern (N.C.)--History--Anecdotes. 2. New Bern (N.C.)--Biography--Anecdotes. 3. New Bern (N.C.)--Social life and customs--Anecdotes. I. Title.
F264.N5H35 2011
975.6'192--dc23
2011017898

For Victor Jones
and
John Green,
historians extraordinaire.

Contents

Preface

Readers of my weekly column in the *New Bern Sun-Journal* have asked when I would put out a "collected works" volume. Here's my answer.

I thought for a while about just how I should present this thing. I've done the column since 2007, and there are well over a hundred to choose from. Should I run the first year's worth as volume 1 and follow it later with the second year's as volume 2? The problem with that is how haphazard the whole thing would look. My columns have been like Kurt Vonnegut's Billy Pilgrim—unstuck in time. One week I would be in 1710, the next in 1922 and the next racing backward to the Civil War. My aim was never chronological. I wished to present readers with a smorgasbord of our recent past.

Some columns appeared as two- and three-parters; sometimes, after periods of subjective somnolence, a new fact or letter would respark my interest on an old topic. Many of the columns I have mined for this book, in fact, have raised further questions in my mind, leading me to dig for and add more information.

And, of course, some of those columns just didn't shine. Knowing that they're immortalized in the *Sun-Journal* archives is punishment enough. I certainly didn't want them in a book. Hey, even Mark Twain had his bad writing days.

So I've opted for a topical collection. I'm choosing certain events and time periods and often melding two or more columns into one. I have chosen both major events that affected our town's history and smaller events that have simply made it more interesting. You will see me mostly bypassing some

Quaint storefronts are revealed behind a banner-bedecked light post on Pollock Street. *Photo by the author.*

of the better-known stories (the Fire of 1922, for instance, or the Stanly-Spaight duel) because other books currently out there cover them already or because I am considering eventually doing a larger work on those individual topics. In other words, our smorgasbord includes main courses, desserts and even hors d'ouevres.

This is especially true in the section on the Civil War. I will mention items that, hopefully, have not been covered too extensively in other books: New Bern's feelings leading up to the war and the involvement of a handful of people during that span of time. If you are new to the Civil War in this town, there are a number of good books that will fill you in. Still, let me give you the extreme gist that will help you understand it right now: We lost the battle, and then we lost the war.

You want to know more than that? Okay, here's the slightly larger nutshell. The Civil War started, officially, with the bombing of Fort Sumter in April 1861. North Carolina seceded from the Union on May 20 of the same year. This means that we weren't in on the opening punch, but you can be sure that we were in the peanut gallery cheering it on and that our governor was busily working to prepare the state for what he knew was coming. This doesn't mean that everyone was for secession, though—New Bern and North Carolina at large had a fair number of pro-Unionists up to and throughout the war.

Our city provided a number of companies of soldiers that would achieve honor throughout the war. None of them was around to defend the hometown, however, when Union general Ambrose Burnside chugged up the Neuse with an amphibious force in March 1862. There were impressive defense works created along the southern side of the Neuse below town, but through a mixture of miscommunication, inexperience and Richmond's obsession that only Virginia really deserved to be well defended, there were not enough Southerners to properly man them. On March 14, they were overrun by vastly superior numbers, and for the remainder of the war, New Bern remained a Union headquarters from which raids were launched.

Because it fell so quickly, much of the historic district was saved—the upside of losing the fight so soon. Because the town was now firmly controlled by a huge Union force, it became a mecca for runaway slaves. Needing a safe place to house them, James City (named after a Union chaplain, Horace James, who orchestrated the event) was established. America's first black regiments were recruited and formed, and from New Bern a number of officers were recruited for the famous Massachusetts Fifty-fourth.

New Bern was attacked by Southern forces several times, but the Yankees held them back each time. There was, however, one big moral victory for the South in its attack on the Union gunboat *Underwriter*.

At the end of the war, citizens returned, and most, though not all, of the Yankees went home. Over time, control of the town was returned to its citizenry. Former Yankees and Confederates met in a grand games competition at the city fairgrounds, and this time the Confederates won. We can't really say that the town went "back to normal," though, as the war had fundamentally changed the nation and its society for all time.

A number of people helped me in the writing of these articles, both through support and advice. I am sure that I will neglect to mention some—my apologies in advance. But among those I need to note, I am grateful to the *New Bern Sun-Journal*, which has been home to my weekly column, and to its editor, Randy Foster, who has been most supportive; thanks also go to the rest of the newsroom gang.

Thanks to Paul Merriman, who read over my material on the Indians and offered advice; to John Leys, who also skimmed for accuracy; and, most especially, to the Kellenberger Room at the Craven-Pamlico Library along with its vastly knowledgeable staff, especially John Green and Victor Jones. Any errors in fact in this volume are mine alone.

Part I

Early New Bern

Tryon Palace as seen from the south lawn. *Photo by the author.*

When Baron de Graffenried arrived, he found a town that had been here before him, possibly for hundreds of years. *Photo by the author.*

They Were Here First

It may seem a little sacrilegious, but I plan to say fairly little about Christopher de Graffenried, our official founder, and John Lawson, the explorer who was also so influential to our founding. Instead, I plan to concentrate on the Native Americans, ending with the story of how the land we call New Bern was claimed from them.

It isn't that the rest of the story isn't worth telling, but it *is* the story about which most readers already have an inkling. Besides, to tell it properly would fill a volume on its own.

A Look at the First New Bernians

New Bern turned three hundred years old in 2010—that may be a hiccup in Europe, where the same paper roll has been hanging in some bathrooms far longer. But three hundred years is downright venerable on American soil. We're even older if you stop to consider the fact that New Bern was a Manhattan Purchase–style takeover of an Indian town that had been here for possibly hundreds of years before. We started out as a Neusioc village named Chatooka, a word meaning "where the fish are drawn out." I am tempted to think of ichthyic psychologists trying to draw a fish out of neuroses brought about by a battered childhood. We will assume, however, that the reference is more about fishermen catching fish.

The Neusiocs were a really small nation—about a dozen warriors and their dependents—when European folk began to inundate the area. But the whole Neuse River was named for them—a river with the widest mouth (six miles) of any in America. That even outdoes that Mississippi River that old Sam Clemens was always gabbling about.

Chatooka was a collection of wigwams, each holding several families. There were wide streets, cultivated gardens and a religious center in which several totem poles were driven into the earth, forming a circular arena. The town was protected with a palisade wall. In the winter months, it was all but abandoned—the strapping young men went off to a winter camp, where they hunted, while the elderly stayed back to hold the fort. Along with the young warriors went their wives, as well as the geekier young men of the town—you know, those clowns who, if you gave them a bow in battle, would wind up shooting themselves or their brother. These guys served as mat makers, potters, wigwam builders and runners.

The local Native Americans had a complex religion and social order. Gaming was popular, laughter was always in the air and they strode about with a stoic, if fatalistic, philosophy regarding every facet of life and death. Now, don't go getting any Disneyesque picture of these people, noble beyond imagining. They most certainly had their flaws, which I will examine. But, as a whole, they were deeply admirable. Which is a good thing. *They* were our founders after all.

We celebrate our birth as September 1710, the month that Baron Christopher de Graffenried's frowning, shocked visage first saw the dire straights of the town that had been awarded him by the lord proprietors and Queen Anne. But was that really the day of New Bern's founding…or of its transition?

We white folk have a curious relationship with Native Americans. We come in, run them off, kill them (intentionally and otherwise) and then name everything in their honor. We decry our past abuse of them, although I have yet to hear of anyone offering to give back Manhattan (or New Bern, for that matter). Every man and his brother claims to be one-eighth Indian, tracing his ancestry to some mysterious Cherokee princess who must have been very loose and fruitful. Numerous women, meanwhile, call on Pocahontas as their direct ancestor, be they as pale as cream and blond as Scandinavia.

Why *do* so many white Americans want so badly to believe that there is Native American in their blood? Is it a subconscious desire for something that most of us can never have: an ancestry that is *truly* American (instead of European)? And why do we insist that our Indian ancestors be princesses? Is this part of our secret and shame-faced love of royalty?

Another habit we have is to look at the broad spectrum of Native American peoples as some kind of united whole. We think various tribes were like various American states, only more nomadic. But they were more like European states than American. Some tribes may have had similar customs compared with others, but their governments and even languages were distinct. Like European nations, they traded, kept their own council and met one another in war.

The current cultural philosophy determines how we look at these people. Back in the days when America saw itself as the product of Manifest Destiny, Indians were irritating squatters, savages to be pushed aside. If you debase a people far enough, you can dismiss them as lesser beings—not even "true" human beings. What is not human you can slaughter without violating your traditional Christian morals. We used the same mind tricks to convince ourselves that slavery was a benevolent condition for blacks. In Australia, this same rationale set up the wholesale slaughter of Aborigines.

Today's New Age spiritualism has brought us to the opposite extreme: Indians are neopagan gods, a superior culture so magically at one with nature that they seem more like the elves of a Tolkien fantasy than anything based in terra firma. Mind you, this doesn't stop us from allowing their reservations to be the most poverty-stricken regions in America. Let's not confuse philosophy with philanthropy.

Who were they really, these people who fished the Neuse before us? Wild savages who slaughtered men, women and children for the sheer joy of butchery? Peace-loving children of the maize who sat about sucking on peace pipes while contemplating grooviness and nirvana? The answers are no and no.

Their culture and technology differed radically from ours, but they were totally human, with the same strengths and weaknesses—a mixture of good and bad, violence and peace—as all mankind. They could be both deeply loving and profoundly cruel.

When you walk through New Bern's historic district, you will see houses that were built as far back as the mid-1700s, a time when there were still a couple of the original De Graffenried settlers hobbling around. You may start to think of the city's *first* homes. What were they like? Well, not brick; that wasn't plentiful back then. Planks? Logs, even?

Actually, they were made of saplings and bark. The first homes, of course, were Neusioc homes—communal wigwams set up in the midst of broad streets and vegetable gardens where cornstalks stood at attention, beans dangled as enticingly as a bean can dangle and squashes grew like fat little yard gnomes on the ground.

John Lawson, the British explorer and, in my humble opinion, cofounder of New Bern, gave extensive descriptions of the life of local Native Americans in his classic book *A New Voyage to Carolina.* (Published in 1709, it's still in print. Don't just stand there. Go buy it.) Living among them for some months, and being their neighbor for some years, he was well qualified to describe New Bern's earliest residences.

They were oval-shaped (Lawson described them as "round like an Oven"), with a framework of long poles (pine, cedar and hickory were preferred). These poles, about the thickness of a man's leg, Lawson estimated, were stripped of branches and bark and heated in a fire for hardening before the broad end was stuck in the ground. The upper ends were bowed and lashed together with elm bark or even Spanish moss. The whole structure was then covered with cypress or cedar bark. There was, of course, a door. A fire was kept in the center of the building, and a hole in the roof let the smoke escape.

The floors were of loose earth, and benches were placed along the walls. On these benches the Indians sat and visited or slept, using mats of thatched rushes as mattresses and animal skins as blankets. Lawson must have visited them in the summer, for he declared these homes to be as hot as stoves: "The Indians sleep and sweat all Night." Several families slept in each one.

They could be alive with fleas as well, but Lawson, sounding for all the world like Gulliver among the Houyhnhnms, declared that they were still better than some European homes. "I never felt any ill, unsavory Smell in their Cabins," he wrote, "whereas, should we live in our Houses, as they do, we should be poison'd with our own Nastiness, which confirms these *Indians* to be, as they really are, some of the sweetest People in the World."

Slaves and Slaving

Unfortunately, Lawson's view was not everyone's. Numerous European settlers saw the natives as perfect "marks" for treachery and easy money. Though Lawson raged against the practice, white traders cheated the local tribes out of goods and—far worse—kidnapped their women, children and young men to sell as slaves. In time, these horrific practices would fizzle out. Native slaves knew the land and could escape too easily, and while they could be trained to many trades, they could not hold up to the heavy labor in intense heat that plantation owners required. Thus, African slavery, already present, grew while Indian enslavement leveled off and then disappeared altogether.

But in 1710, when the New Bern settlers arrived, it was a raging problem. We don't know who, if any, among our city's founders captured Indians for this purpose. One suspect was William Brice, a trader and fighter who had already settled in the area when the Swiss and Germans arrived (he would prove to be quite a headache for Baron de Graffenried). Some of these slaves ended up in places not too far away—Lawson referred to Indian slaves he had observed in Charleston—but most were sent to the northern colonies. One of the most fascinating testimonials to North Carolinians making slaves of their neighbors comes from, of all places, my old stomping grounds of Pennsylvania. It happened on June 10, 1710, a couple of months before De Graffenried and his Swiss showed up. The Tuscaroras appeared before the Susquehannocks (a tribe to whom they were related) at Conestoga and met with John Ffrench and Henry Worley, who represented the English Crown. Representing the Tuscaroras were Iwaggenst Terrutawanern and Teonnottein (makes your tongue numb just thinking about pronouncing names like that). Representatives from the Iroquois nation in New York (more relatives of the Tuscaroras) were also on the scene.

The Tuscaroras hoped that their tribe could find asylum in this Quaker-run land. Life had become dangerous and unbearable in Carolina, and William Penn, after all, had made himself known as a friend to the natives. They presented the settlers with several wampum belts symbolizing the troubles that they'd had with their wily, pale-skinned neighbors.

Each belt represented a different segment of the tribe: the old women who wished to be able to fetch water and wood in safety; the children who wished to roam and play without fear of being kidnapped and sold as slaves; the young men who wished to hunt for their families without fear of being killed or enslaved; and old men who wished for woods that were as safe as their walled villages.

The Pennsylvanians were sympathetic but distant: if the Tuscaroras wanted to settle here, they had to secure a certificate of good behavior from the North Carolina legislature—not a likely event, since the Carolinians would not want to see the lucrative fur trade pack up and head north.

The Tuscaroras did not get that certificate; we have no evidence that they even tried. Sullenly they gathered in their villages and debated in their councils. A year and three months after the Pennsylvania meeting, they used the only option they felt was left to them and went to war.

To give the devil his due, we must point out that at least some Indian tribes had been making slaves of their own enemies for years. These slaves were made to do menial tasks in the villages such as weaving mats, collecting firewood and helping to set up winter hunting camps. It was not the kind of hard labor that Europeans often put their slaves to—after all, the Tuscaroras had no sugar plantation death farms like the British and French controlled in the Indies nor even the backbreaking tobacco, cotton and rice plantations that these strange local white men ran.

Like slaves anywhere, the Indians' slaves were the lowest members of their society, beneath warriors, laborers, children and women. Undoubtedly they put up with their share of ridicule and torment. The most horrific part of a slave's life, though, was his initiation.

According to John Lawson, Indians maimed their newly captured slaves, cutting the skin at their toes and then peeling it back halfway up the top of their foot. The front half of a foot was cut off, and the flap of skin was wrapped around the stump to heal. Naturally, there was no medication to ease the pain. The theory was that, so hobbled, a slave would have a rough time running away. Those who did could be easily tracked via the odd footprint they left. Even so, a few managed to find freedom.

Sometimes a captured enemy was spared the loss of half his feet, only to be sold, instead, to white traders. This makes it seem, on the surface, hypocritical that Indians would so angrily denounce their own enslavement by the Europeans. But there were differences, the main one being that the Tuscaroras enslaved their enemies only. It was a "booty" kind of thing, the spoils of battle. I have not seen any sources describing the enslavement of women by the Indians, at least not in name. Perhaps female survivors of the losing village were absorbed into the tribe as reluctant wives.

The European settlers, however, had been capturing young men, women and children of the tribes who were their friends and trading partners. If sin has degrees, theirs was certainly the more serious one.

Manhattaning Chatooka

Baron Christoph von Graffenried (who liked to refer to himself by the more French "Christopher de Graffenried") first stepped foot into the town of which he was officially founder in the early fall of 1710. His German settlers had preceded him, and he found them in desperate straits. He also found a Neusioc Indian village he hadn't expected. As he pondered how to deal with it, he went ahead and built a cabin. Judging by his own account of New Bern's

A Baron Christopher de Graffenried bust on display on Pollock Street next to city hall. *Photo by the author.*

founding, written in later years to absolve himself of guilt in the town's failure, I should guess that he built it within sight of the Indian village's walls.

Lawson urged him to run the Indians out. At least, that is what De Graffenried tells us; this seems to seriously counter what we know of Lawson and his respect for the Indians. Perhaps De Graffenried is being a little creative with facts or at least taking some conversations out of context. If Lawson did, however, urge him to run them out, one wonders what must have been going through his head to make him act so contrary to his nature. If the Indians got wind of this story, it probably added to their anger when they captured and slew him a year later.

In any case, De Graffenried wrote that he could never simply chase them off. He decided, probably sometime later in 1710, to offer the Indians a buyout for Chatooka (the baron called it Cartouca) and resettle them ten miles up the Neuse. The chief of the town, King Taylor, agreed to meet and discuss the matter.

What is your image of this grave ceremony? Wizened old men sitting about a fire, passing a peace pipe while they give metaphysical speeches? Solemn nods, agreements and a ceremonial conclusion? If so, think again. The whole thing went off like a bad comedy, and the Neusioc came out the worst for it.

The day of the meeting was set, and King Taylor (whom De Graffenried kept calling a "kinglet") showed up with seventeen men—warriors, most likely. We know from Lawson's writing that Chatooka was a small village of only twenty-odd families, so the representatives made a sizeable percentage of the population.

One can get an idea of how De Graffenried looked upon the coming proceedings from his description of King Taylor's dress: "The kinglet dressed himself in his best, but in such a grotesque fashion that he seemed more like an ape than a man." Those Indians went to an open field nearby and sat in a circle, waiting for De Graffenried to join them.

Aiming to impress, the baron showed up in "whatever would glitter most," probably a rather elaborate suit of clothes given him by the lord proprietors when they'd named him landgrave a year before. One wonders if King Taylor and his boys later snickered about *his* get-up.

Scorning having to sit on the ground, De Graffenried ordered a chair brought, which was done *post-chaise*. Standing beside him was an interpreter, "a Savage who spoke English well." The Switzer opened the ceremonies by handing out gifts—"several presents of little value," he noted.

The baron's description of the day suggests that the meeting followed Neusioc custom: De Graffenried offered his reasons as to why it was wise for King Tayor to sell off his ancestral grounds and move upriver. When he was done, any Indian who wished to speak was allowed to do so. A number did, and at least a few were quite opposed. De Graffenried later admitted, "[T]o speak without partiality they had better reasons in their opposition than I."

Nonetheless, Manifest Destiny was knocking at the noble's door. "We came to an agreement," he later wrote. He carefully presented his offer: "[T]o the king two flasks of powder, holding four pounds, a flask holding two pounds, and with that 1,000 coarse grains of buckshot; to each of the chiefs a flask of powder and 500 lead shots…rather coarse…After that I had them drink well on rum, brandy distilled of the settlings of sugar, the ordinary liquor in this country, and the agreement was made."

In other words, he bought the land with seventy-eight pounds of gunpowder, 8,500 "rather coarse" lead shots and one thousand coarse grains of buckshot. And this is assuming that he counted all seventeen men with Taylor as "chiefs" and that they each received four-pound, rather than two-pound, flasks. To get them to buy a deal like that, he got them roaring drunk.

At some point during the proceedings, De Graffenried had some major trouble from his own man Friday. Franz Louis Michel was a Swiss explorer of some note. A partner with De Graffenried in this whole venture, Michel had on prior trips explored Virginia and Pennsylvania in search of possible sites for Swiss settlement. Though fond of him at first, De Graffenried later wrote that God might just judge and slay Michel if he didn't experience a major conversion in his life.

He certainly was less than admirable this night. He had been drinking with English friends somewhere nearby, De Graffenried wrote. All at once he appeared at the ceremony, staggered up to King Taylor, grabbed his headdress and hurled it as far as he could. He then entered the council circle, grabbed one of the more eloquent men who had spoken in opposition to selling the land, dragged him aside and "gave him several blows." The Englishmen dragged Michel away while the king suggested heatedly that "if the Christians made peace and their alliances after that fashion he did not want to have anything to do with them."

De Graffenried struggled to bring things back under control:

> *I did not fail to answer him that he ought not to pay attention to what a brute, controlled by the power of liquor, had done, that I would reprimand him vigorously for it and I would even send him far away, that he should not insult them more, that they should rely on me assuring themselves that I would never do them injury so long as they were good neighbors with me.*

Apparently the address eased the Indians' minds; rum was procured and all drank heartily. That night, while the baron was asleep, Michel snuck out again, found the orator and beat him until other Indians subdued him yet again. The baron marveled that they didn't beat Michel for his repeated offense.

De Graffenried did, he said, address Michel on his behavior. He sent him on one or two minor explorations and then finally sent him to Philadelphia on assignment to secure mining rights in Pennsylvania from William Penn. It sounds as though he was sending him away to appease the Indians, but by his own admission, this was not so: "Several days after [Michel's] departure, the king with some of his Indians came to find me. Not knowing that for other reasons I had this Mr. M. leave, he evidenced much joy that I had delivered them from the dangerous man."

New Bern was now in white hands, and the Neusiocs, recovering from the effects of the spirits, soon resented the trade they had made. Numerous seeds had been planted that would grow into a tragic war.

Addendum

"No good deed goes unpunished," *Vanity Fair* editor Clare Boothe Luce once wrote. As evidence of this, let's investigate the eventual fate of the little tribe who aided the Tuscaroras in their meeting with the Pennsylvanians.

This tribe was the Susquehannocks, once a fairly powerful Indian nation. By 1710, their numbers had been ravaged by disease to the point that they had, at most, a few hundred men and women. By this time, they primarily resided in a village called Conestoga in Lancaster County. Many of them were practicing Christians.

For some years after the failed meeting at Conestoga between the Tuscaroras and the Pennsylvanians, the Susquehannocks continued to live peaceably with their neighbors, although disease kept whittling their numbers. By 1763, only twenty were left. Prejudice and an unrelated Indian rebellion would finish those.

It was in 1763 when an Ottawa leader named Pontiac made history with his rebellion against British rule in present-day Detroit. The rebellion even spread into Pennsylvania. Fort Pitt (now Pittsburgh) was besieged, and its defenders attempted biological warfare: they exposed blankets to smallpox victims and handed them over to Indian representatives during a parley.

The fighting never got near Lancaster County, and the Susquehannocks never involved themselves in it, but that didn't stop the Paxton Boys, a group of vigilantes who used a Descartes-esque formula ("I think it is, therefore it is true") to declare that the Susquehannocks were sending information to the rebellious tribes. On December 14, 1763, they marched on the village and, finding six Indians, promptly murdered them. The government placed the remaining fourteen in protective custody in a Lancaster jail. The Paxton Boys then broke into the jail and murdered the rest, making the tribe extinct.

None of the Paxton Boys was ever brought to trial.

What's in a Name?

It took years of phonetic evolution before we settled on what—exactly—was our name.

Named after a Swiss city, the word "Bern" in New Bern means "bear." It's a symbol you're not likely to miss in a stroll downtown, from the bear over the chamber of commerce sign to the pair sticking out of city hall, the bruins emblazoned on our police cars or in the form of concrete, iron and wooden sculptures nearly littering the town. The meaning behind "New Bern" is pretty simple. But the spelling? That's a little trickier.

Baron de Graffenried neglected to legally register a spelling for the town. The result was a series of linguistic fits. For the first 170 years, no one had any idea how to write it out. If only Mr. Webster had included us in his

City hall stands behind a street banner displaying the appropriately spelled name of New Bern, North Carolina. *Photo by the author.*

dictionary, but no, we were left to our own devices.

Early on, the single-word moniker of "Newbern" was king. Some men wrote "Newberne," with that silent "e" at the end. The effect was more intellectual than verbal. Say it, and you'll hold your pinky up as you sip your morning Earl Grey.

The city's first printer, James Davis, printed it as one word, sans the "e." Our founding fathers, whose records and letters are so carefully preserved in the colonial records, spelled it every way imaginable—one word, two words, with a silent "e" and without. Even North Carolina's most capable colonial governor, William Tryon, spelled it as both one and two words.

Virginia newspapers preferred one word, and so did Mark Twain, who wrote a delightful and true story about a freed slave woman's experiences in our town during the Civil War entitled—are you ready?—"A True Story." George Washington showed some creativity in his journal when, on April 20, 1791, he managed to spell it two different ways in two consecutive sentences: "Newbern" at first and then "Newburn," as though the town were on fire.

The Yankees who controlled New Bern during the Civil War also preferred the single-word name. Most soldiers' letters' return addresses carry "Newbern," as do many of the period's maps. An 1862 map, however, describes the "Battle of Newberne" (such highfalutin cartography just had to have been the work of a Bostonian).

It was not until 1897 that someone finally got around to settling the city's spelling in the lawbooks. Ignoring the popularity of the single-word name (yes, they actually had the audacity to go against Mark Twain), the final spelling split the word and dropped the "e." We are New Bern to this day and for the foreseeable future.

Like the constant shifts in its spelling, New Bern's personality has been ever-changing: bucolic fishing village, war-torn settlement, maritime center, colonial capital and occupied military center of operations. The twentieth century saw it turn from a major lumber town to a sleepy, decaying southern town, awakening at last, yawning, to the benefits of its history for financial and cultural gain. As you can see, there's plenty of fodder to fill this book.

Mr. Tryon Comes to Town

You've seen his house, now meet the colorful gentleman who became North Carolina's most successful colonial governor.

I have a special fondness for William Tryon. Not only do I find the cumbersome Brown Bess musket of his day more interesting than the deadly-accurate Enfield of the 1860s, colonial politics interest me more, too. Besides, I portrayed the governor at Tryon Palace for a couple of years, greeting folks in the council chamber and chewing the fat about the colonies and the king. I began to feel like I personally knew the fellow.

The reconstructed Tryon Palace, built to the specifications of William Tryon's original structure. *Photo by the author.*

Strangely, I have never written an article about Mr. Tryon and the Battle of Alamance. So you won't read much of Alamance here (in the suggested reading section at the end, you will find the title of an excellent and brief book). We'll instead look at the rise of his Palace and a few of the lesser-known but still important moments of his mercurial life.

Birth of His Excellency

Each June 8, New Bernians everywhere should turn east, face the Tryon burial site at Twickenham, England, and sing "Happy Birthday." Sing quietly, though—someone owns the rights.

It was on that day in 1729 (the same year North Carolina officially became a Crown colony) that William Tryon was born at Norbury Park, Surrey, England. Without him we would have no Tryon Palace or Tryon Palace Seafood in town and certainly no Tryon Park in beautiful downtown New York. See them all and tell folks I said, "Hey."

Much of the aura of New Bern today is built around this colonial governor. He actually spent most of his term in the former governor's residence at Brunswick, near Wilmington (the town was burned down by the British and never rebuilt). He lived in town for only a year, and yet that one year was highly influential in our state's history.

His family, probably of Dutch descent, was long in the tooth in England. His ancestor, Peter Tryon, a wealthy Flemish man, fled the tyrant Duke of Alba in 1562. Other descendants had been in the British Isles since 1066. Through his mother, Lady Mary Shirley Tryon, he was of the seed of Queen Elizabeth's pet, the Earl of Essex.

His father, Charles (whose portrait hangs in the master bedroom at Tryon Palace), would die young, in his forties. William had several siblings: Charles, Robert and James were older; and Mary Sophia and Anne were younger. That's about all we know about his childhood. He was well educated and soon developed a love of books (in New Bern, he collected what was, for the time, an immense library). He took to the military, becoming lieutenant of the First Regiment of the Foot Guards in 1751 (were its guns primed with Desinex powder?), and he was later promoted to lieutenant colonel. He showed bravery in action in 1758 during the Seven Years' War, when he helped oversee a withdrawal from the beaches of St. Cas Bay, where the British were overwhelmed by French defenders.

A secret of politics is to "marry well." Although he sowed some wild oats, resulting in a love child named Mary Stanton (the mother's name was

Elizabeth), he settled down and married the heiress Margaret Wake in 1757. While he remembered Mary in his will, he was entirely loyal to Margaret throughout their lives. It was through her connections that he became governor of North Carolina.

Hero on the Seas

Thirty-six-year-old William Tryon arrived in Wilmington, North Carolina, to take a post as lieutenant governor on October 10, 1764. He was probably pretty proud of his passage, as well he should have been. It had been quite an interesting voyage.

He'd been a passenger on Captain Veriner's snow (pronounced *snoo*), the *Friendship*. With him were his beautiful and ambitious wife Margaret, their three-year-old daughter, also named Margaret, and the bachelor John Hawks, who would later build Tryon Palace (and, later still, support the Revolutionary cause).

One day early in the voyage, a cry came from above: "Sails! A sloop!" Sloops were small, one-masted affairs. This one (the *Tyge*) was lying dangerously low in the water. Its master, John Barns, told Captain Veriner that it was floundering with five feet of seawater in its hold. For two days the crew had been desperately bailing and pumping, but the sea was gaining and the sloop was losing. The crew had already thrown more than half of its cargo overboard in an attempt to lighten it and buy time. They begged Captain Veriner to take them all on board. Veriner sent his carpenter across, but there was nothing he could do. Still, the island of Madeira was nearby; could the sloop make it that far? Barns was willing to try, but for safety's sake, Mrs. Sealy and her son were sent to the *Friendship*, being ignominiously lowered into the longboat that would transfer her by being tied to a line.

One wonders what three-year-old Margaret's thoughts might have been as she watched her father and others hauling a soaked, seven-year-old, wide-eyed boy over the gunwale. Did Mrs. Tryon hurry the mother and son below decks, shouting orders for blankets and hot tea, while Miss Margaret clung anxiously to her skirts, stumbling along and staring in wonder?

On deck, Tryon and Hawks kept vigil with Captain Veriner and the crew. Madeira was hours away. Could the floundering *Tyge* last?

At midnight, Barns fired his guns as a signal—the *Tyge* was going down and *fast*. Veriner launched the longboat and, in four trips, ferried the remaining passengers and crew back to the *Friendship*. New Bern's *Carolina Gazette* later reported that Tryon "exerted himself greatly, and was very anxious the whole Time for their Safety."

The crews and passengers watched as, with the high waves beating and washing it, the *Tyge* was pulled to its watery grave. Our greatest colonial governor watched, satisfied in the knowledge that he had done all that he could to help save lives.

The Death of Governor Dobbs

William Tryon was the kind of guy who jumped right into things. He had believed that when he arrived in North Carolina he would find Arthur Dobbs, the man he was replacing, practically standing with his baggage on the docks. Tryon's sharp military mind was ready to move forward with the business of running the colony—he had plans upon plans in his head, not the least of which was establishing a permanent capital for the colony (to this date the business of government had moved cyclically from town to town). He'd even brought along an architect to plan the official building.

Dobbs was an ancient man at seventy-six years. He was worn out, no longer loved by his constituents, who had taken to mocking him because of Justina Davis, his fifteen-year-old bride. The old duffer had made a buffoon of himself, men grumbled. Many of the more austere, elderly plantation men cast a libidinous eye at the maiden and secretly ate their hearts out.

Hated and worn out or not, Dobbs wasn't ready to go. Tryon was flabbergasted. "I waited on Governor Dobbs and informed Him of the Honor His Majesty had conferred on me," Tryon wrote in a hot letter to the Earl of Halifax:

> [T]*he Intelligence of my Appointment, he said had, reached him two Months before my Arrival and that upon Receipt of his Leave of Absence in July last, he had wrote to his Friend Lord Egmont, to request a Sloop of War to carry him home; this gave me an Opportunity to ask him when he proposed to take his Departure for England, he told me he should stay till next Spring, to the Middle of April, or beginning of May; this I own was a Thunderbolt to me, and I hope will be an Apology for me to Your Lordship for the Earnestness with which I expressed my Apprehensions to your Lordship and Mr. Sedwick of this Event...I shall...be inducted into an office which is likely to be burdensome to me this Winter, for want of Employ.*

John Adams once declared of the vice presidency: "My country has in its wisdom contrived for me the most insignificant office that ever the invention of man contrived or his imagination conceived." Apparently, Tryon felt the same regarding the post of lieutenant governor.

But Dobbs was unruffled by his protégé's impatience. He was used to having his own way. Over the next few months, Tryon was introduced to the legislature, and then, wanting "Employ," he and his wife toured their new colony over the winter months. We might think that winter was a strange time to travel, but in Tryon's eye, the summer was just too far away—and a deadly season for being on the road, with yellow fever around. Spring, also too distant, promised only swollen streams to ford and quagmire roads of mud.

His travels did him good, giving him important contacts and information that would keep him in good stead over his coming six years of rule. Still, he itched to control the governor's seal.

Finally, Dobbs set a date for his departure, April 1765, though he described it to Tryon as a "leave" rather than a resignation. Having the typical old-guy's disease of "I can do it myself," he insisted on doing much of his own packing. The doctors were not happy and tried to slow him down; the old Irishman ignored them. "His physician had no other means to prevent his fatiguing himself," Tryon wrote to the Earl of Halifax, "than by telling him he had better prepare himself for a much longer Voyage."

On March 25, while packing books, he was struck by a seizure. Two days later, in his young bride's arms, he died. Justina wrote a letter to inform Dobbs's sons in Ireland: "I have lost one of the best and tenderest of husbands and you a kind and most affectionate father." The girl would ultimately turn into something of a gold digger, but her words seemed sincere at the time.

We don't hear much these days about Dobbs, but he was a fascinating man. A naturalist, he is credited for his work (back in his Irish days) with bees; in America, he is credited as the European who discovered and named the Venus flytrap, a plant native only to the Croatan Forests near Havelock, as well as a few other isolated coastal spots. He had also been a persuasive advocate of the search for a Northwest Passage around North America. He was buried on the church grounds in Brunswick, where he had lived (he had earlier removed the government from New Bern's shoulders because he didn't like the climate there). No clergyman could be found to conduct his funeral, and today no one knows the location of his grave.

Though he did not leave an impression on colonial history and politics like Tryon's, he was still a capable leader and a warring adventurer who left his imprint on the science of botany.

Great Wolf

Tryon's multiple baptisms into governorship were severe: the aftermath of a duel between a sailor and his captain (the loser being a relative of Margaret Tryon's), the whole bitter business with the stamp tax and the early stirrings from the Regulators (tax protestors who would tail him throughout his gubernatorial career). Though much of the coast loved him, colonists deeper in the colony's interior connected him with massive spending and with casting a blind eye to the corruption of local officials (the former has at least some basis, in his building of the elaborate Palace, but corruption was an issue he worked doggedly to solve for years, if with limited success).

One of his most admirable achievements served, in his time, to further alienate his interior subjects. This event culminated on June 1 and 2, 1767, when he arrived in the hamlet of Salisbury, where he staked his colony's peace on a border treaty with the Cherokee Indians. The British saw the Appalachians as a kind of permanent barrier to mass settlement by their European subjects; they made a convenient line of demarcation between them and Native Americans. Of course, the land-hungry colonists resented these imposed boundaries—one reason why Indians tended to side with the British during the Revolutionary War.

For some years now, whites had been filtering into Cherokee territory, building homesteads on their ancestral hunting grounds. The Indians were getting rather miffed.

John Stuart, the king's agent for Indian affairs in the Carolinas, had pressed South Carolina to set an official border over which whites could not encroach. He hadn't come to North Carolina yet, but Tryon thought that he had a fine idea. Indian trade was advantageous for both sides; Indian wars were advantageous for neither.

Tryon convinced the Assembly to advance him £100 toward his expenses. He loaded up some wagons with gifts and supplies, and then, with his good friend Edmund Fanning, his most trusted officer Hugh Waddell (a Wilmingtonian) and two regiments of militia from Rowan and Mecklenburg Counties, he began his westward trek. He left on May 19. He would not see home again until June 13.

He later described the costumes that his militiamen wore: "Each Man had his Rifle Gun, and their general Uniform and appointments were a Carters Frock, Indian Match Clouts (in lieu of Breeches) Moccasons (for shoes) and Woollen or Leather Leggins; the latter were necessary to prevent the bite of the Snakes of which We saw a great Plenty." It is interesting to note where Tryon set his emphasis via capital letters in that last sentence.

His party traveled over the border into northern South Carolina, where, at the Reedy River, he met with Cherokee chief Ustenuah Ottassatic (thankfully for our Anglo tongues, he was also known by the name Juds Friend). Feasting, gifts and negotiations began on June 1. Tryon gave a speech to his Indian guests, concluding that he would "most faithfully adhere to [the boundary] and…pursue every measure that may strengthen and brighten the Chain which holds fast that Peace and Harmony which at present happily subsists between us."

"We have met here and smoked together as brothers," Juds Friend stated the next day. "The white People and ourselves should be all one," he added, but then he included a hint of wariness regarding the trustworthiness of white men's treaties: "I hope our Talks will be straight and Right."

Surveying work began on June 4, and the governor hung around for two days to watch it unfold. On the sixth, he headed for home.

On June 13, an agreement was signed noting that the border would run northeast from the northwestern corner of South Carolina, passing over the top of Tryon Mountain (roughly the Asheville area) to Colonel Chiswell's lead mines and into Virginia.

The Indians honored Tryon with a new name: Great Wolf. He arrived home, weary after an 843-mile trip and minus his horse, which had been stolen somewhere along the line.

It is unlikely that a boundary aimed at aiding the Native Americans was popular with most people, even on the coast. The Tuscarora War may seem a distant event to us, but it had ended only fifty-two years before Tryon's trip—there were survivors of the September 1711 massacres who were still alive.

Tryon was under direct orders from England to honor the treaty: "I must particularly recommend to you, that this necessary Work may be executed with Candor and the Stipulations observed with good Faith," the Earl of Shelburne wrote to him from Whitehall in England. "For nothing can more effectually conciliate the minds and Affections of the Indians, than a Measure which must convince them that we mean to protect them in the peaceable Possession of those Lands which are necessary for their actual Subsistance."

It was a border that would be honored, for the most part, until Andrew Jackson arrived in the White House in 1829 and instituted the Trail of Tears.

How Tryon Palace Came to Be

Here is the story of how one of the finest buildings in colonial America came about. Hints of Tryon's plans to construct what would become known as "the Palace" began showing up even before Governor Dobbs died.

Take, for instance, a Moravian document written on March 24, 1765, four days before Dobbs's demise, noting that a "young man" in their community had appeared, "sent by Lieutenant-Governor Tryon to get all kinds of seeds from us for the plantation which Tryon wishes to lay out." (The Moravians had a settlement near present-day Winston-Salem.)

Dobbs's body had barely grown cold before the new acting-governor (he would not receive his official title until July) was scratching off a letter to the board of trade, hinting at his future plans:

> *I spent two months in a tour thro' this Province, and am determined in my opinion that the public business of it can be carried on, no where with so much conveniency and advantage to far the greatest part of the inhabitants as at Newberne, a town situated on a neck of land at the confluence of the rivers Neuse and Trent.*

An initial "Bill for erecting a convenient building within the Town of New Bern for the residence of the Governor or Commander in Chief for the time being" was passed on December 2, 1766—but it was only an initial bill. This is government, remember. Nothing takes place quickly. The bill was revised and offered up over and over again.

On November 12, Tryon's good friend from Hillsborough, Edmund Fanning, sponsored a bill requesting £5,000 for the construction of this "Edifice," to be collected through poll taxes. The whole ceremony of presenting the bill seemed like an exercise in patience. "Mr. Fanning moved for leave to bring in a Bill," the minutes of the Assembly report. So he was told to go *get* the bill. He brought it, read it "in his place and delivered it at the Table." There the clerk read it all over again. The Assembly passed it and sent it on to the Governor's Council.

The next day, the bill was presented again:

> *Received from the Assembly by Mr Fanning and Mr Elmsley a Bill for erecting a convenient building within the town of New Bern for the residence of the Governor or Commander in Chief for the time being. On motion read the first time and passed.*

A view of Tryon Palace's cantilevered stairwell. *Photo by the author.*

It was still floating around between the houses on the fourteenth when Tryon pressed his case before his Governor's Council:

> *His Excellency then acquainted this Board that an intention hath been communicated to him for carrying a Bill into execution thro' this General Assembly for erecting a Publick Edifice at New Bern for the Governor for the time being, and as this measure has been recommended from the Crown, and will be a means of removing those inconveniences Governors of this Province have laboured under for want of a Proper House of Accomodation, particularly during the setting of the General Assembly and as such an Establishment has been made in almost every Colony of this Continent for their Respective Governors, His Excellency recommends all due support may be given to this Bill by His Majestys Council.*

Note the subtle suggestion that this whole bill was not his idea. Also, the traditional argument that every parent on earth knows so well: "But everybody *else* has one!" Over the next few weeks, the bill was brought up, amended, read, passed and handed over to the other house at least four times. Finally, on December 1, 1766, it was read as passed in its final form to the governor. He had his £5,000 and permission to turn John Hawks's architectural mind loose on what we all now know and love as Tryon Palace.

Within a month, though, the governor realized that his £5,000 would prove to be woefully inadequate, as he wrote to the Earl of Shelburne in January 1767:

> *The Act for erecting an Edifice for the Governor and his Successors was carried by a great Majority of the Assembly. The Five Thousand Pounds voted for the House and Offices will be short of the Expence of erecting them.*

Still, he was excited that the project was approved. He continued to the Earl of Shelburne:

> *Mr. Hawks has contracted to finish the Whole in Three years from the laying the first Brick which I guess will be in May next; He goes soon to Philadelphia to hire able Workmen, as this Province affords none capable of such an Undertaking.*

Hawks had been busy with the Palace long before this. His first drawings had been completed by December 29, 1766. The design was Georgian, with its obsession toward balance and favoring "a London vicinity house."

Master Hawks bore a lot of responsibility. He was not only to draw up the plans of the building but also to travel the seaboard seeking the laborers and materials that were wanting in rural North Carolina. He had to purchase the land, hire the men and see to the delivery of supplies. The house, eighty-two feet wide by fifty-nine feet deep, along with its stables and kitchens, was to be ready for occupancy by the first of October 1770.

On February 23, Tryon was sending plans and elevations for the Earl of Shelburne to give to the king, as well as bringing up, again, the overruns he was expecting:

> *My Lord,*
>
> *I have the Honor to transmit to Your Lordship the Plan and Elevation of the Edifice with the Offices to be erected at Newbern by Virtue of*

an Act passed the last General Assembly of this Province. The Expence of finishing this building in the plainest Manner is estimated at Ten Thousand Pounds Sterling, I shall therefore at present order only the Body of the House to be Constructed and defer going upon building the Office till the General Assembly grants a further supply, which I have reason to believe is the Intention of the Public.

He made a successful a pitch for another £10,000 from the Assembly in December 1767. In January, he wrote to Lord Hillsborough, boasting about the mansion's progress:

It is with a singular pleasure I am able to inform Your Lordship the House building at Newbern for the Governor of this Province is covered in & roofed. The Plumbers work was executed by an able Hand sent purposely over from London; He made use of eight Ton of Lead. The Frames & Window Sashes are fix't up, and the joiners now at work on the inside of the House. Both the Wings, or Offices, are likewise roofed and Shingled, a covering when well executed & Painted, more beautiful than Slate or Tyle. The Sashes for these Offices are come in from England and will soon be fix'd up; four of the principal Chimney pieces are arrived also from London, with the Hinges, Locks & other Articles necessary for the finishing this much admired Structure; As I think there is great elegance both in the Taste and workmanship in the Chimney Piece for the Council Chamber, executed by the able artist Mr. De Vol, I take the liberty to inclose You the description.

That enclosure was instrumental in obtaining good duplication within the rebuilt Palace of today and is often referred to by guides giving tours of the chamber almost 250 years later:

A large Statuary Ionic Chimney Piece, the Shafts of the Columns Sienna and the Frett on the Frieze inlaid with the same. A Rich Vaze and Foliage on the Tablet; Medals of the King and Queen on the Frieze over the Columns, the mouldings enriched, a large Statuary Marble Slab and black marble Covings.

He went on to request that the king pay for "necessary interior conveniences and Ornaments," namely furniture. Politely, George III refused.

Occasionally, Tryon's well of building funds from the Assembly dried up. At such times, he borrowed from colonists—so much from one businessman, Samuel Cornell, that some historians kid that it was really Cornell's Palace.

Though detail work was incomplete, the edifice was finally ready to receive Governor Tryon and his two Margarets in June 1770, a full five months ahead of schedule. He held a grand open house late that year, on December 5, the same time he was holding an emergency session of the General Assembly to address growing problems with the Regulator movement. There is an interesting irony here, for that movement had gained its greatest impetus through the heavy taxes forced on subjects to pay for the Palace. Tryon took special care to thank the colony for this "gift" with which many were not happy:

> *I gladly embrace the Opportunity offered Me of making my Grateful Acknowledgements to the Country for their Gift of this very Elegant and Noble Structure for the residence of myself and Successors in Administration. A Palace, that is a public Ornament and Credit to the Colony, as well as an Honor to British America. A Construction, I am persuaded, from the Strength and Choice of its Materials, the Integrity, Diligence, and Ability, of the Architect, with the skill of several Artificers employed, will remain a lasting Monument of the Liberality of this Country.*

As you stroll the rebuilt Palace today, you can see what a monument to luxury it was and can contemplate its place in the role of American dissension and independence.

The Hurricane of '69

Tea taxes, Regulators and Cherokees weren't the only things with which Governor Tryon had to deal. Sometimes, it seemed, even the weather rose up to get him.

If you can't deal with a day or two straight of several inches of rain and more than seventy-mile-per-hour wind, you really shouldn't live in the coastal Carolinas. I'm sure that in some obscure language "hurricane" and "North Carolina" mean the same thing. A big one—a *really* big one—came in September 1769. It had no name (naming them didn't officially start until 1953), and we have no wind measurements, but eyewitness descriptions suggest it was one of the worst to hit North Carolina in its colonial history.

The whole thing started with a sign—or so Governor Tryon believed, observing from his Brunswick home "a blazing Planet or star" whizzing through space late in August. He later conjectured, in a letter to the Earl of Hillsborough, that this might have been the hurricane's cause.

The storm wreaked havoc from Cape Fear to Williamsburg. John Smith, a New Bern businessman, noted that rain began to fall about 6:00 p.m. on September 7. He recorded the rising gale, an interesting description of the circular habits of a hurricane: "[T]he wind [was] at N.E., and so continued until 9 or 10, then shifted to S.E. and about two in the morning the tide was 10 or 12 feet above its usual height; about this time the wind shifted to S.W. which occasioned the tide to fall, or it would have destroyed this town, which is already near effected."

New Bern is not exactly known for its high elevation (some of us fondly think of speed bumps as our own Appalachians). Smith's waterfront home had a cellar that was stacked with wine, rum and sugar. During the storm, it was completely flooded. Every item was "either stove to Pieces or floated away," according to New Bernian Thomas Howe. Meanwhile, Smith stood on the first floor above, listening to the growing trauma of the storm:

> *My dwelling-house, and Mr.* [Samuel] *Cornell's, which joins it…were almost washed down; the lower floors of both fell in, the other parts are miraculously standing on parts of the cellar wall…At one in the morning the water was 18 inches on my lower floor. I broke through into Mr. Cornell's garret, with my wife and three children, three of Mr. Cornell's youngest daughters, and many others in both families, amounting in the whole to 28 souls, and escaped out of Mr. Cornell's back door, with the children on our shoulders, and the water up to our chins, wading near 250 or 300 yards to the highest ground, in order to preserve our lives, which under the provident care of Almighty God was most fortunately effected.*

Smith lost more than his house: "[M]y wharfs, warehouse, its contents of corn, salt, sugar &c my dry good store totally gone, with about 800 £ sterling of goods in it; my books, bonds, notes, papers, paper money, specie (some part of which I found again) together with several other houses, and their contents of considerable value."

James Davis, the colony printer and publisher of a weekly newspaper, saw his business wash away. "Mr. Davis's House [is] a mere Wreck," Howe wrote to the governor. "His printing Office [is] broke to Pieces, his Papers destroyed and Types buried in the Sands." Davis and his children spent a number of days combing the shore for those types, and his paper was temporarily shut down.

"Sixty odd houses are totally destroyed," Smith wrote, "and a large number of others much damaged."

"Newbern is really now a Spectacle," Howe observed. "Her Streets full of the Tops of Houses, Timber, Shingles, Dry Goods, Barrels & Hogsheads, empty most of them, Rubbish &c &c: in so much that You can hardly pass along."

It is amazing how few lives were lost. "Five white people and two black people are drowned," Smith declared, with "many others bruised in the ruins of fallen houses." Tryon identified four of those victims as "Mrs. Johnston and Mrs. Pape with their two Children…drowned or killed by the ruins of these Buildings."

Governor Tryon foresaw a bigger, related disaster: "It is imagined that as the Corn was within six Weeks of its Maturity, the Planters may save about half a Crop, but they have no hopes of recovering the Rice lying at this period under Water from the [freshets] that this Gust occasioned. The Country will I fear be greatly distressed this winter for Provisions."

The recurring visitation of storms helps us to remember that the past is as close as the present. "A few days ago so flourishing and thriving," Mr. Howe concluded, "it shows the Instability of all Sublinary Things."

The Good, the Bad and the Ugly

We are orderly beings. We like our heroes tall and straight and our villains stunted and crooked. We really don't have time to juggle with seeing humanity on either side. Take Governor Tryon. Supporters love him. Detractors hate him. In the nineteenth century, he was considered the ultimate tyrant. Today, the spirit of a resurrected Palace and thriving tourism have some almost seeing him as a guy who could stand in line for the Pope—if only those British rulers hadn't been so darned antipapist.

The truth is that he was a capable man of his times. Some things he did were really good, and a few were bad. Some of his "badness" was a little chilling any way you look at it, but much of it only looks bad because he was on the side of the British.

His correspondence reveals a number of his characteristics. Learned and eloquent, he was a decisive man who knew exactly what he wanted and had no qualms in going for it. He had a sharp wit and could be self-deprecating at times. He obviously adored his daughter.

Tryon sometimes did the right thing despite opinion around him. Settling the Cherokee boundary was decidedly unpopular with colonials who lusted for their western lands. When the Stamp Act was coming into effect, Tryon attempted to mollify Carolinians by hosting a large dinner for a number of merchants, promising to seek special status for North Carolina from England (since paper money was a problem here). He offered to personally pay the stamp tax on any legal documents for which he would collect a fee and also for the colony's taverns. No one was interested in biting this carrot, but still it was sincerely offered. He was in no position as representative of the king to say, "By George, you're right! George is wrong! By all that's just, let's ignore him!"

He presented arguments to his Assembly that tax collectors were dishonest, over-collecting and shortchanging the government of what was legitimately owed. He protested growing problems with counterfeiting. A devout churchman, he worked hard to find new blood from England to shepherd the colonists and labored for better compensation for those clergymen.

During a particularly harsh winter in New York, when he was governor there, he ordered free firewood to be given to the poor.

He had a love child in his early days (not a good thing) but acted responsibly about it, remembering this daughter in his will (certainly not a bad thing).

No one can question his abilities as governor, and he was at least competent as a military man. A rumor printed in the *Williamsburg Gazette* suggested that he was taking over as commander of the king's forces in America, and he carried himself heroically in battle during the Seven Years' War.

That is the yin. Now here's the yang. Tryon was not lacking in faults and acts of cruelty. One could write whole chapters on the following events, but for now let's settle for this abbreviated version.

First, there was the sad case of Chief Justice Charles Berry. This judge, considered by his peers to be a man beyond suspicion or compromise, oversaw the trial of Captain Alexander Simpson. Captain Simpson, sympathizing with colonists' abhorrence of the Stamp Act, killed his lieutenant, Thomas Whitehurst (a relative of Tryon's wife, Margaret), in a duel over the issue. When Simpson was acquitted in the trial, Tryon called Berry before the council and showed his extreme displeasure.

Berry was so distraught over the possibility of censure, or even impeachment, that he committed suicide, ripping his bowels open with a penknife. "Tryon was…the murderer of this talented and amiable man," declared nineteenth-century historian John Hill Wheeler with, perhaps, a little too much certainty.

As any fan of Jimmy Carter's awful historical novel *The Hornet's Nest* knows, Tryon hanged half a dozen of his Regulator prisoners after the Battle of Alamance (and another half a dozen were pardoned). He also personally shot and killed an escaping prisoner just before the battle. One cannot technically fault the governor for these acts, as he was within his rights. But one *can* question his hanging the prisoner James Few, who was not even sane, immediately after the battle and with no trial at all. A 1905 history claimed that Few was engaged to a woman who had been seduced by one of Tryon's favorites, Edmund Fanning, and that Fanning had particularly pressed for his death—although that is the only source I've seen for this angle on the story.

Tryon's most notorious act took place some years after he left North Carolina to become governor of New York. The Revolution had been raging for a couple of years, and Tryon was then leading a force of men against the colonials. In the early morning of April 27, 1777, he ordered his men to burn to the ground the Patriot town of Danbury, Connecticut, which he had occupied, as a lesson to all who would dare oppose the king.

The lesson backfired. Razing the town only fired up Patriot souls, and soon three thousand citizens flocked to join their cause.

Part II

Antebellum Tales

Hay House, part of the Tryon Palace Historic Sites and Gardens tour. *Photo by the author.*

ANOTHER STANLY DUEL?

In 1802, John Stanly found notoriety by killing former governor Richard Dobbs Spaight. He wasn't the only Stanly to strut at the "field of honor."

In the antebellum South, a man who was called a snake or a liar, or who had experienced the indignity of someone tossing a bit of cake into his teacup, was ready to take or give a life to defend his honor in a duel.

Firearms were more popular than swords. This was because it evened the field: any fool can aim a pistol and squeeze the trigger. Pistols also improved your chances to survive—not even the best shooter was guaranteed to hit his target. A smoothbore pistol sending that ball rattling and banging down the barrel and out into the open air was no sure thing. You may as well blindfold David, spin him until he is dizzy and still expect him to fell Goliath. As often as not, a shot or two was fired, and honor was declared as served.

John Stanly, a noted lawyer and congressman, advised his brother to take part in a duel that was brought about after someone playfully tossed a piece of cake. *Lithograph by Pendletons, Boston, from a painting by Ford, Series P2, North Carolina Collection Photographic Archives, Wilson Library, University of North Carolina at Chapel Hill.*

All right, I exaggerate. Still, while a duel could be a pretty nasty, and sometimes fatal, affair, it wasn't the absolute harbinger of death that the movies teach us. Imagine that, Hollywood being wrong.

New Bern had a major duel: Congressman John Stanly slew ex-governor Richard Dobbs Spaight in 1802 over politics and insults. The state was outraged—Spaight was a popular old codger, one of the signers of the United States Constitution—and dueling was outlawed in the state as a result.

Actually, the Stanlys were dueling machines. They were the sons of John Wright Stanly, a Revolutionary War Patriot whose privateering fleet made him rich and whose destiny with yellow fever made all of that wealth pretty much pointless. John Wright had married the beautiful daughter of a local Patriot, and she died about the same time he did and of the same dreaded disease. This left the Stanly boys orphaned, without any famous parents to set moral boundaries to their heroic notions.

In the chilly month of February 1813, William Gaston, close friend of John, decided to entertain his associates by inviting them to a fine party at his home. John, at the time, was training his younger brother, twenty-four-year-old Thomas Turner Stanly, in the art of lawyering, and so the youth was invited along.

Also at the party was Louis D. Henry, the young apprentice of the prominent attorney Edward Graham. Louis and Thomas knew each other. Typical youths, they tended to joke and sport with each other. Apparently, also like typical youths, they were girl crazy, and the lovely young Lucy Hawkins of Warren County was in their midst.

One silly girl, two hot-tempered young men and one party (complete with cake) equaled one dead Thomas. Let's see how it all went down: Thomas, in a jovial mood, winged a bit of cake at Louis. It landed in his teacup, splashing his vest. Lucy looked at Louis and, laughing, asked, "Are you going to stand for that?"

Testosterone reared its ugly head. Before you knew it, Louis had challenged Stanly to a duel. Thomas sought the advice of his brother on the matter. John replied that accepting the challenge would be a very fine thing. Thomas probably saw it as a chance to match his brother's reputation.

A day was set: Sunday, on Valentine's Day, ironically enough. To sidestep the anti-dueling laws, Louis and Thomas crossed into Virginia via Gates County. There is no official record of just where the duel took place—not surprising, since the Virginia government wasn't overly friendly about gentlemen popping one another off, either. But we can take an educated guess: the Great Dismal Swamp.

This fetid region was the scene of a canal that had been started in 1792 (and completed about 1805). It was a speakeasy of sorts for duelists. Isolated yet accessible, a haunt of runaway slaves, it was rarely visited by lawmen. The swamp was such a popular setting for the matches, in fact, that the Lake Drummond Hotel, when built there in 1829, actively advertised for duelists to come.

We don't know if Lucy watched the event. For his second, Thomas brought George Badger, a man who would develop quite a reputation and name for himself later on. Louis chose Dr. Boyd as his second. Another physician, Dr. Scott, came along to patch up any nonfatal holes.

Duels were fought in ordered rounds, carefully following the etiquette of the game known as the *Code Duello*: the duelists drank a toast, possibly shook hands, lined up back to back and marched their paces. They turned and, upon a given order, fired—or took turns firing. The men usually stood sidewise, making a smaller target (very fat men were wise to avoid dueling). If one man fired first, he could not do the sensible thing and run for cover; he had to stand there while his opponent popped off a shot. If the first round missed—and more often than not it did—the seconds would see if "honor had been served" or whether apologies would be given to end the duel. If not, they fired again and repeated the steps until they wore out and gave it up or someone got wounded or killed. On rare occasion, things would really heat up, and the seconds would start banging it out as well. Most often, the first shots were enough; indeed, sometimes the men purposely fired into the air, and it all turned out to be a dramatic sham in the name of honor.

Such was not usually the case with the Stanlys. A duel was a duel, and someone was supposed to die. Louis and Thomas made their paces, turned and fired. Somehow Louis's first shot buried itself into Thomas's right side, piercing his heart, and the younger Stanly dropped dead on the spot. The victor fled to New York but later returned to North Carolina, where he pursued a successful, and even brilliant, political career. He died in 1846 and was buried in Raleigh.

You'd think that Thomas's death would have cooled the Stanly blood, but it did not. Another brother, Richard, dueled with swords in the West Indies and was slain. Even John Stanly's son, Edward, according to some historians, tried his hand, against Alabama congressman Samuel W. Ingle. Edward's second, interestingly enough, was Jefferson Davis. Edward and Ingle both missed on the first shot and had enough sense to stop.

I wonder if it had anything to do with cake.

THE WAR OF 1812

Otway Burns and the Snap Dragon

Sometimes it was called "Mr. Madison's War." President James Madison had begun it, but a large percentage of America was against it. New Bern seemed to have as many people in opposition to this war as it had men in favor of it. The parallels to Vietnam are interesting, including the war's unkempt and uncertain outcome (a tie in this case, more or less, with our greatest victory—New Orleans—coming after the war had technically ended). And like any wars, there were men whose patriotism was increased by their ability to financially profit from victory.

Dr. Edward Pasteur was a powerful man. Though he held no public office, he carried great weight that went beyond his medical degree. He was a fancier of horses (one, Snap Dragon, he had received from John Hawks, architect of Tryon Palace) and had captained the Newbern Light Infantry Company at least as late as 1807, when he was mentioned in a *Newbern Morning Herald* article, drilling his men near St. John's Masonic lodge.

Pasteur had made himself somewhat notorious near that same lodge in 1802 when he'd served as second for the ill-fated Richard Dobbs Spaight in the Stanly-Spaight duel.

Perhaps he was inspired by the thought of the glories and wealth of John Wright Stanly, privateer of the American Revolution. He traveled to New York to purchase a privateering ship. His choice of captain, Otway Burns, a noted seafarer from nearby Carteret County, went with him. They picked a four-year-old, 147-ton ship called the *Zephyr*, applied for a letter of marque (governmental permission to act as privateers against the nation's enemies) and then renamed their ship after Dr. Pasteur's horse.

Well, we are not *certain* that he named it after his horse; it might have been named after a game that was popular with sailors on shore leave. You have seen boys playing slapping games to see who can tolerate the most pain from the other—this was down that same masochistic alley. In "snap dragon," a glass of brandy was sprinkled with raisins, and as they floated on the surface, the brandy was set afire. The player had to pluck and eat the raisins without getting burnt. Obviously, a lot of scorched fingers ensued. Possibly, Burns thought that this might be a good-luck emblem for a ship that aimed to "burn the fingers" of British merchants. Personally I think the horse story is more likely, but possibly both the horse and the game played into the name. History is often guesswork.

On August 27, the letter of marque arrived, and they sailed for New Bern to outfit their ship and land a crew. Fifty shares of stock were sold to investors from New Bern and other nearby towns.

The *Snap Dragon* already came with a swivel gun and some gun carriages (rather useless without the guns), as well as some of the hand weapons (cutlasses, boarding pikes, pickaxes and pistols) that made boarding a ship such a quick and violent event.

This model of the *Snap Dragon* is on display at the Beaufort Maritime Museum. *Photo by the author.*

For some reason, Burns seemed to have a difficult time with the local leaders, who, despite the example of John Wright Stanly, took a low view of privateering. Probably they were men particularly opposed to the war. One underhanded stunt of the townsmen was to convince Burns's crew to take out loans and then swoop in and arrest them for debt. Captain Burns would spend several years in his later life as a cooler head in state government, but in 1812 his temper was short and his eloquence physical. When a number of constables came sailing out to board his ship, he simply sank them. When a local attorney referred to him as a "licensed robber," he came ashore and threw the man into the river so he could take his case to the fishes. It was probably with a sigh of relief that these politicians watched the *Snap Dragon* head for sea and fame on October 14. The war was four months old.

The *Snap Dragon* was one of the fastest ships afloat, and under Burns's skillful hand, it outmaneuvered and outran a number of British pursuers in its time. Burns quickly gobbled up treasures and made the ship's investors rich.

As a child, local historian John D. Whitford knew Burns and listened to some of his stories. In his rather rambling history, *Home Story of a Walking Stick*, Whitford related a tale in which Burns, running low on ammunition in a fight, loaded his guns with sail needles captured from an earlier prize. Once this was fired into the enemy ship, the crew quickly surrendered.

Burns commanded the *Snap Dragon* for three cruises, menacing British shipping along the Carolina coast and from the banks off Newfoundland to South America. That third voyage, in 1814, included an unfortunate event for Burns. Whitford described it:

> *While cruising near the shores of South America he overhauled and tackled a ship that after a hot contest surrendered. Burns then, frenzied with wine and victory, placed a red signal flag he held in his hand in the rigging of his vessel to scare the vanquished. They understanding it to mean piracy and butchery, as they should without knowing their captor's motive, renewed the battle for their lives and, fighting like demons, beat off the Snap-Dragon. With the foremast shot away and otherwise so badly crippled was the vessel that Burns was fortunate to escape in any way, as capture would have meant the Yard arm for his neck, if not for all the crew.*
>
> *Subsequently it was ascertained the ship had a valuable cargo for London and two hundred and twenty five thousand silver dollars on board. The Captain on his arrival at his port of destination reported the occurrence with the remark—"The privateer had caught a goose but did not know how to pick it." The writer has a copy from the original log giving all the particulars of the battle, the repairing of the vessel and the cruise until the return to New Bern.*

Such a prize slipping through his fingers was unforgivable to the investors. They fired Burns and named William R. Graham captain. The *Snap Dragon* left the port of Beaufort for the last time as an American craft on May 26, 1814.

Graham started out well enough: his ship came upon the British schooner *Linnet*, which was carrying fish, oil and beef tongues (talk about a lovely meal) off Halifax. But his glory was to be short-lived. The British had sent the man-of-war *Leopard* disguised to look like a merchantman. Graham fell for the ruse and drew in close to board. Suddenly the *Leopard* let loose with a broadside, killing a number of men on the *Snap Dragon*, including one of its chief officers, Lieutenant Decokely.

A furious fight followed, but the *Snap Dragon* was undone. It was captured and its crew sent to sit out the war at the notorious Dartmoor Prison in Devon, England. The *Snap Dragon* was sold to merchants in New Brunswick, who pulled a tit-for-tat scenario and made it a privateer against American interests. I have seen no record of its success (or lack of it) against its former masters.

This memorial, featuring a cannon removed from the *Snap Dragon*, was placed over Otway Burns's grave by his grandsons in 1901. He is buried at the Old Burying Ground on Anne Street, Beaufort, North Carolina. *Photo by the author.*

Perhaps the more experienced and wily Captain Burns, who better knew his ship, might have been able to elude the British trap, and perhaps Edward Pasteur stayed awake a few nights regretting his poor character judgment.

Civilian Casualties without a Fight

In America's first two wars, New Bern got off pretty easy. The town was occupied for a day or so during the Revolution, during which Loyalists murdered the Patriot Alexander Gaston (father of Judge William Gaston) and burned some boats, but that was it. The War of 1812 was even kinder: not an enemy's sole tramped our streets.

It says something about our town's greatness, though, that even without any British troops in the place, we managed to suffer a casualty in that war. And that, oddly enough, was suffered by the same guy who'd lost his father in the Revolution.

By then, William Gaston was a prominent man, deeply loved and admired. He had a thriving law business and powerful friends and had helped found a library in town in 1803 (head librarian Salmon Hall received a salary of fifty dollars per year). He was also a freshman congressman known for his friendship to the downtrodden and the freedmen. Like his father he was a Patriot, though he was no friend to the prowar administration in Washington.

Gaston had married the former Hannah McClure on October 10, 1805, just a year after the death of his first bride, Susan Hay (they'd been married for only eight months when sickness took her). Hannah and William were deeply fond of each other, but his Congressional duties kept him away for months at a time. Hannah, who was soon pregnant, wrote often, and her letters spoke frequently about the children and their fondness for their missing Pa. "They are well and speak constantly of you," she wrote once, "Margaret has had several crying spells when she thinks she sees you and then is not noticed [by the mistaken man]."

New Bern was militarily vulnerable. On July 17, 1813, word arrived that the British had been sighted off Ocracoke—they were headed for land, and it was certain that they were going to march on New Bern! Hannah was visiting a neighbor when someone knocked, and the announcement was apparently made in a tone of dread and hopelessness, for she hurried immediately home and spent the next several hours pacing about in a growing panic. About 8:00 p.m., she was seized with convulsions brought on by her mental trauma. By 3:00 a.m., she and her unborn child were dead. Gaston heard of it two days later and hurried home to his devastated family.

The British never did come.

God and Mr. Clark

Elijah Clark was quite a man in his day. He built carriages, owned warehouses and served the town as mayor and sheriff. But his proudest accomplishment was a church.

It was May 11, 1809, a Thursday, and his friends were at his home for a visit. For some hours they sat in the parlor, plotting and praying. The main topic of discussion was something near and dear to their lives but something they didn't have: a church. A *Baptist* church. Tradition says that this meeting took place at the Elijah Clark House, a gambrel-roofed home on a triangular lot at the north end of Middle Street. Clark did not purchase the home until 1812, but that doesn't absolutely rule out its happening there. His grandson, John D. Whitford, said that it took place here. It is possible that he was renting the home when it did.

In that day, only two denominations were up and running in town: the Episcopalians (founded as Anglican in 1715) and their theological

The Elijah Clark House on Middle Street as it appeared about 1905. *Courtesy First Baptist Church, New Bern.*

relatives the Methodists (the local congregation was founded in 1772). Back in 1741, several Baptist men petitioned the General Assembly to allow them to build a church. They were given an emphatic "No" and then were publicly whipped and jailed for their efforts. In 1809, things were calmer; the freewheeling Methodists might laugh, and the prayer book–loving Anglicans might turn up their noses, but at least no one would park a whipping cart by Elijah's door.

Like many young congregations, these Baptists started as a house church, with Elijah's parlor as a sanctuary. By 1812, they had raised a boxlike building of their own. It was located at the corner of Johnson and Metcalf Streets (St. Cyprian's stands there today). It was a drafty place in winter, according to local wag (and Presbyterian) Stephen Chester:

The Baptist Barn comes next to view,
Where winter winds turn noses blue,
And shiv'ring devotees retire
Right glad from worship to the fire.

The musical program was neat. Instead of the traditional piano or organ, the Baptists landed a Franklin harmonica. By harmonica, I do not mean that little perforated bar we sway to when Bob Dylan tunes are on the radio—this harmonica consisted of glass bowls in a wooden case. The bowls were tuned by holding varying amounts of water. The player wet his fingers and played the rims. Volume was occasionally an issue, but only in large halls. Though no longer played, that harmonica, purchased in 1811, is still held by the church. Ask nicely and they'll probably let you have a look.

Enough noses had turned blue by 1845 that a new building was contemplated. Elijah and his grandson, John D. Whitford, took a trip to New York and adapted plans from the Madison Avenue Baptist Church. The result was standing on Middle Street by 1848. The cost? A cool $12,000. Over the years, this interesting brick-and-stone amoeba has grown to cover quite a bit of land.

I gather from Mr. Whitford's writings that the sermons could sometimes be fiery and eventful. One pastor, while preaching, was distracted by a little boy in the front row turning the leaves of a book. The minister grew so furious that he ended the whole service and sent his congregation home.

Whitford complained of the same church nuisances that people take issue with today: latecomers, noisy children and (with a wink) fashion belles: "It is, if reprehensible, a pretty picture as she trips gracefully along the aisle, nearly filling it with the feathers and flowers and ribbons shaking on her hat, so jauntily fixed over her smiling or frowning face. Then, too, it gives the other sisters already there something to praise or condemn as to her taste in dressing, when they get home."

First Baptist Church as it appears today. *Photo by the author.*

First Baptist spent the Civil War as a commissary. In 1948, it hosted a visit from President Harry S. Truman, an acquaintance of the pastor.

It makes for a fine walk today to admire the curious angles and spires of First

Baptist and then wend one's way to the original "meetinghouse" of Elijah Clark at 616 Middle Street a few blocks away. A little concrete boy with a pole used to be seated on a bench in the side yard, apparently thinking about fishing and remembering when this place was the residence of fishers of men.

In his business life, Elijah was for a time a chair maker, as well as a merchant and the operator of a brickyard near Lawson's Creek, according to architectural historian Peter B. Sandbeck.

In his writings, John Whitford couldn't say enough about his grandfather. He admired Elijah's piety but winked at his youthful failings; he joked how, as a young man, Elijah got himself in trouble a number of times by sneaking off to the horse races on the Sabbath. On the more "moral" side, he described Elijah's efforts to win at politics in a very worldly world.

Perhaps you've heard the story of the fine Christian man who decided to run for Congress. He visited his elderly pastor and brought up his vision. "I won't vote for you," the pastor warned severely.

"Won't vote for me?"

"You'll *never* receive my vote."

"But why?" the young man asked, flabbergasted. "Don't you think we need a Christian in the halls of Congress?"

"If you *make* it to the halls of Congress," the pastor snapped, "you won't *be* a Christian anymore!"

Elijah Clark, respected businessman and societal pillar, served some years as the county sheriff. It was a public office, but not one for which the public voted—in the early days, that position was chosen by the county magistrates. But sometime after 1830 (I will guess in 1835, when the state constitution was changed), the county sheriff became a publicly elected post.

Clark had a number of supporters who were, shall we say, less spiritual than he. They quietly warned him that the machinery of public elections was oiled with free liquor. If the devout Mr. Clark were not willing to make this one compromise and spread the spirits, he would at least need to turn a blind eye while his friends lubricated the electoral process for him.

Clark was incensed. "Let me be defeated!" his grandson reported him saying. "I will never let myself, or through you or others, treat [voters] to spirituous liquors, or promise any man office who in my opinion has not the *moral* character to hold it as the law designed!"

"But Elijah!"

"No! I will not!"

Thus the elections ran, and so did the spirits—from the opposing ticket. For Elijah Clark, the voting box was almost as dry as he was himself. Climbing onto a bit of a "demon's rum" soapbox himself, his grandson declared that his vote was "opposed with unrelenting bitterness" by the town's majority of hard-drinking voters.

It wasn't only city- and county-wide offices that relied on the whiskey vote. New Bernian William Salter Blackledge ran his successful race for the Seventeenth Congress (1821–23) by spending $2,740 out of his coffers for liquor alone—a princely sum in that day.

But let us not feel too badly for Mr. Clark. He remained a successful businessman and spiritual leader throughout his life and spent many years as the city's treasurer, as well as landed his name in the footnotes of history as a church founder. And finally we must remember that, for him at least, his electoral loss was a moral win. As his grandson noted, "[W]as it not a victory for his Church as well as for a Christian man?"

The Athens of North Carolina

You will usually hear New Bernians refer to ourselves today as the "Athens of the South." I even have a small production company that goes by that name, but historically, we were more humble in our self-adulation. We settled for just being the "Athens of North Carolina."

A lot of that title has to do with our history of local theater, which goes a long way back. Governor William Tryon, in a letter to the bishop of London, mentioned a troupe of actors under Henry Giffard. Tryon hosted a circus, too. Okay, the "circus" was really the General Assembly, but if you've ever seen a General Assembly in action, you'll agree we're just talking semantics here.

New Bernian James Iredell witnessed an apparently "execrable" performance of Moliere's *The Miser* in 1787, according to Alan D. Watson's history, and in the 1790s, Thomas Turner's distillery on East Front Street served as a theater, complete with a gallery for blacks.

From its earliest days, St. John's Masonic Theater has been a center of stage and theater. It is still used that way—it is one of the oldest operating theaters in the country.

Nineteenth-century New Bernian Stephen F. Miller fondly recalled "Mr. Herbert's Theatrical company of 1823": "Mr. Herbert played Richard III, and was quite successful in genteel comedy in the character of an old man…Mr. Drummond was most effective in gay scenes, representing fast young men." In Goldsmith's admired comedy, *She Stoops to Conquer*, "Mrs. Waring made a brilliant display as widow Cheerly." Thomas Pasteur was so intrigued by her performances

J.H. Bailey ran a popular theater in New Bern at the eve of the Civil War. Here a show is advertised "under the patronage of the mayor and fifty leading citizens," from the January 1861 *Newbern Daily Progress.*

that he followed her to Charleston, never to find his way back home.

He also referred to a "Thespian Society...composed of young men whose representations I also witnessed." James W. Bryan, for instance, "did full justice to the young Duke Avanza, in the costume of a Spanish cavalier." Miller also recalled Alexander F. Gaston, who "sustained a character in knee-breeches. Persons who have seen the figure of that gentleman, stooped in the shoulders, yet six feet and four inches high and his knees bent inward, can well imagine the comic effect he produced on the audience. It was the climax of the entertainment."

A *New Bern Spectator* article on September 5, 1834, mentioned performances by visiting actors from Philadelphia, Baltimore and Petersburg, Virginia—august presences who made "Mr. Conner's company...decidedly superior to any that has performed here for several years."

In the late 1850s, the Bailey Troupe was doing regular performances that seemed quite impressive. For instance, this advertisement appeared in the *Daily Progress*:

Bailey Troupe!

This popular company will give a series of
Entertainments
In the Theatre,
In Newbern,
During the Christmas Holidays,
Commencing on

Tuesday Evening, Dec. 25, 1860:
Consisting of
New Songs
Fancy Dances, Comedies,
Dramas, Farces, Negro
Melodies and
Dissolving Views
Tickets of admission 50 cents Children
and Servants 25 cents
Doors open at half past 7 o'clock, performance to
Commence at 8

"For the energy which Mr. Bailey is devoting to our Theatre we hope he will meet a generous response from the public," wrote the editor on January 7. "The Company are rehearsing new pieces, and negotiations have been commenced with talented *artistes* at a distance, so that we may look for a brilliant and successful season."

Mr. Bailey was never content to present only a play. "Incidental to this piece are several beautiful dances, by Misses Emilie and Fannie, with many new tricks of legerdemain," J.H. Bailey proclaimed through the newspaper on February 9 of that year. "During the Evening New songs, dances, &c., &c. The whole evening concluding with a laughable farce." And the main show that night? *Our American Cousin*, the same play Abraham Lincoln would be watching, five years later, while John Wilkes Booth stood outside his balcony seat door.

Finest Hotel in the South

A lot of important stuff happened in 1855, or was about to. In engineering, the London became the first train in the world to cross a suspension bridge, spanning the river near Niagara Falls and designed by John A. Roebling, who would later design the Brooklyn Bridge. In literature, Thomas Bullfinch finished his *Bullfinch's Mythology*, much to the delight of scholars and the abhorrence of their students. Whitman's *Leaves of Grass* hit the streets, a poetic masterpiece and a commercial failure.

In his musty Cambridge dwelling,
in his study in the twilight,
Henry Wadsworth, called Longfellow,
wrote the poem Hiawatha.

An advertisement for the Gaston House hotel, from the 1858 *Newbern Journal*.

The hot dog was three years old (no evidence that it had made it to New Bern yet). Commodore Perry's trade agreement with Japan had been signed for a year (a New Bernian, William Roberts, was on Perry's ship. He brought the first spider lilies to America). Missourians had just flooded Kansas, illegally voting a proslavery legislature into that wannabe state. Elevators were two years down the road, and Isaac Singer was even now eyeing that wondrous sewing machine invention of Elias Howe, envisioning its manufacture for the masses.

Meanwhile, on April 23 in New Bern, the Gaston was opening for business. We're not talking a small potato in the historical sack here. The Gaston (named for a prominent judge and congressman) would become known as one of the finest hotels in the South. Proprietor T.L. Hall was enthusiastic in an announcement that ran in the *Newbern Journal* on April 15, 1855:

> *As the entire House is finished and furnished in a superior style, with everything new, adapted to the comfort and convenience of guests, the Proprietor feels that he can give entire satisfaction to everyone who may favor him with their patronage.*
>
> *As to the Table…our almost daily communication with New York will enable it to get its supplies from the North, as well as from our home markets.*

That access to northern cuisine would probably be a big boon to the Yankees who would claim the place during the Civil War.

During that war, the hotel underwent its first name change. "The Union Hotel was formerly the Gaston House," Unionist John Hedrick wrote from there in a letter to his brother in 1862, "as the old sign over the door, which has been imperfectly covered by the paint of the new one, indicates."

In 1870, Samuel Rogers Street Jr., who would build a fine, still-standing home on Pollock Street in 1882, owned it. By the turn of the century, when lumber baron James Blades manned its helm, the business had gone back to its old moniker of Gaston Hotel. A 1910 publication, *Souvenir of New Bern, North Carolina*, described it as "the best hotel in the state," noting that it had recently undergone a $100,000 renovation. That's about $2,273,881 in 2011 dollars.

The publication went on to claim that it featured sixty sleeping rooms, from a commodious fourteen by eighteen feet to an enormous thirty-five by fifty feet. Hot and cold water, electric lights, private bathrooms with porcelain tubs and steam heat, and in a bit of PR that echo today's standards, these rooms were "not excelled in their sanitary qualities, this being one of the particular points of the management to look after." No roaches here, by golly. If there *were* any, they were *clean*. The kitchen, the advertisements bragged, "is supplied with the latest improved cooking appliances, bake ovens and steam tables." "The promptest service" was guaranteed.

Photographs of the period show some fine rooms and dining rooms; polished spittoons are strategically placed to keep the tile clean.

Over time, the memory of Judge Gaston faded, while the star of Governor Tryon (thanks to the Palace restoration) shone again. As a result, the Gaston Hotel became the Governor Tryon Hotel sometime in the mid-twentieth century. It was still considered one of the finest in the state. It might *still* be if it weren't for one of New Bern's grandest and oldest nemeses: fire.

The blaze began about 1:00 a.m. on November 2, 1965, in one of the guest rooms. It quickly spread, and by night's end half of a city block had gone down.

Eleven pieces of fire equipment lined the streets to battle the conflagration, while one hundred firefighters hosed, whacked and rescued away. Along with New Bern's finest were fire companies from as far away as Kinston.

The twenty-seven guests were all rescued, some carried down ladders. Two were taken to the hospital—one because of her "advanced years" and the other "because she was hysterical," according to reports.

A food store, a bakery, a beauty shop and several other offices housed on the hotel's first floor went up with everything else. Total damage, adjusted to

2011 dollars, was about $6.8 million. It was declared the worst fire since the 1922 fire that destroyed one-fourth of the town. The famous hotel was never rebuilt but was allowed to fade into fond memories.

The Gaston Hotel does have one curious descendant. Mr. Street's old Pollock Street digs have been transformed into the Aerie Bed-and-Breakfast. It's nice to see things following in the family business.

Will the Real "Equalizer" Please Stand Up?

A popular advertising slogan of the nineteenth-century said: "God made men. Samuel Colt made men equal."

This Connecticut Yankee in King Lincoln's Court sold more handguns for the Civil War than anyone else. New Bernians love to claim everything as having happened here first, but seeing that Mr. Colt was a northerner tried and true, it pretty much guarantees that the honor of the revolving gun invention doesn't go to us, doesn't it?

Well, not necessarily. Enter John Gill, a New Bernian with incredibly bad luck. A man of many talents, he was a locksmith, a watchmaker and a goldsmith and silversmith (Tryon Palace houses some of his work). According to the U.S. Patent Office, John in 1829 (or in 1820, if we are to believe our native, nineteenth-century historian John D. Whitford) invented a revolving-chamber gun. It was far more ambitious—or perhaps "cumbersome" is the word I'm looking for—than Colt's would be, for it boasted fourteen chambers. Whitford remembered seeing and handling the gun before the Civil War. When that war broke out, the gun was still here, but marauding Yankees came upon it while raiding homes after their residents fled—exit one historic artifact from New Bern.

Despite his many talents, John was not a man of money, and his friends advised him not to waste his funds on a patent; nonetheless, he was determined to protect his invention. A few years later, about 1836, he went by boat (trains from New Bern were a dream of the future then) to Baltimore, but before he could finish his trip to D.C., he fell violently ill.

While recovering, a friend convinced him to let him borrow the weapon. We don't know what happened during that time, but when Gill finally got well enough to knock on the patent office door, he found that Samuel Colt had just beaten him to the punch with a patent for his own six-shooter.

Gill was convinced that somehow, during his illness, Colt had gotten his design from the friend and stolen it. Whitford himself declared this as if it was fact: "John Gill [was] the inventor, it is claimed and justly it is believed, of what is known as Colts revolving gun. Out of the credit and profit of the invention Gill was tricked while visiting Washington to obtain the patent."

Gill kept that gun for many years and showed it to Whitford, who remembered seeing it on many occasions. After his death, it was passed on to the Matthews family, who kept it until 1862, when the Yankees arrived.

No wonder natives only refer to Yankees with the prefix "damned"!

The Coming of the Railroad

When I mentioned that trains were a dream for travel for Mr. Gill in 1836, I didn't mean that they didn't exist. They'd been around for about eleven years.

Inventor George Stevenson was running his first locomotive through the English countryside in 1825; a year later, Quincy, Massachusetts, set up the first rail line in America. One of our country's most famous locomotives, the John Bull (a Stephenson model, imported in crates from England) arrived in New York in 1831. It was the first locomotive to have that eye-catching feature, the cowcatcher, in front.

An early twentieth-century photograph of a train crossing the Trent River trestle near downtown New Bern. The arrival of the railroad was an important boon for the city. *Courtesy William Perkins Library Special Collections, Duke University, Durham, North Carolina.*

For Mr. Gill, though, a trip to the U.S. capital via New York or Quincy would have been badly out of his way. He needed a railroad in North Carolina, and there simply weren't any that close to New Bern. There was one—a nine-mile stretch—running from Petersburg, Virginia, that dipped into North Carolina near Halifax. The Wilmington and Raleigh Railroad was chartered a year later (*chartered*, not built) but would have also been well out of Mr. Gill's way.

Although merchants and farmers around New Bern dreamed of a railroad of their own, it didn't even begin to become a reality until 1848, when the Atlantic Railroad laid a line from Raleigh to Goldsboro. New Bernians perked up and began to seriously seek one of their own. ("Newbern is sinking down, down, down [without one]," a fellow wrote in the local paper, according to historian Alan Watson.) A town meeting was called to raise subscriptions for a line in 1849. They came up with $70,000, a princely sum, in just one convention a couple of years later.

Finally, in 1854, the Atlantic & North Carolina Railroad was chartered, with New Bern as its headquarters. Twenty-eight-year-old New Bernian John Dalton Whitford was elected president of the board in a meeting held over July 20 and 21; he held that post for the next thirteen years. Two-thirds of the railroad company was owned by the state.

Once completed, the rail would connect New Bern to Goldsboro in the west. To the east, it would run to Beaufort's busy harbor. Well, almost. The railroad stopped opposite the Newport River's wide and marshy mouth from Beaufort, and so the town of Morehead City—named after John Motley Morehead, former governor and a key player in the railroad's formation—grew up around it (incorporated in 1860).

The company broke ground in 1856 and purchased engines from locomotive works in New York, Philadelphia and New Jersey, naming them after local leaders, such as the Dr. Hawks (after Dr. Francis Lister Hawks, a noted cleric, historian and grandson of the colonial architect John Hawks), the William Gaston (after the state Supreme Court justice) and the John Stanly (probably after the congressman of the same name, though possibly after his father, a privateer in the Revolution). The first train crossed the Trent River railroad bridge on February 25, 1858, and the line was opened for passengers from Goldsboro to New Bern on April 29. It wasn't until June 7 that passengers were able to travel to Beaufort, however.

The Goldsboro–New Bern junction was running in late April and was celebrated with grand opening parades and feasting, the likes of which New Bernians had not seen in many years. The committee to plan the celebration numbered fifty people, with John D. Whitford as chairman to arrange a ball and William H. Oliver to chair the committee on entertainment. He went full throttle, sending to New York for white granite plates and other table service. Years later, Oliver recalled the massive efforts he went through:

> *I soon secured about two thousand pounds of fresh meats and about one thousand bushels of oysters, which constituted the substantials. The celebration was to be on Thursday; the fresh meats and oysters were to be delivered on Tuesday. On the day they were delivered the weather turned extremely warm, and we were afraid the meats and oysters would be spoiled. With fear and anxiety we went to bed on Tuesday night, as the weather still continued very warm. Imagine the relief the next morning to find a sudden change in the weather, and quite a heavy snow had fallen, and everything was safe. Almost every household was ready to commence cooking and all went at it willingly. Mr. Sebastian Bangert had baked a vast number of loaves of bread, which with a number of barrels of crackers was used. A number was engaged in making and baking a vast number of peach and apple pies. Knowing that our western friends could not raise as fine sweet potatoes as the east, I bought a boat load of fine yam potatoes and they were put in Mr. Bangert's bake oven on Wednesday night and baked to perfection; they were spread on the tables and greatly enjoyed by many who had never before had* [sic] *eaten the yam potatoe.*
>
> *Seven long tables had been erected; they were covered with nice white cloth and on them were placed the crockery and the glassware. Probably there never before or since in North Carolina were more imposing tables set for a public entertainment. On Thursday morning all was bustle, everyone busy, and a host of persons were bringing the provisions which had been cooked by almost every household in Newbern. The town was soon full of people, it being estimated at eight thousand as visitors.*

Among these visitors were militia, bands, locomotives from other railroads, fire companies and enough militia units to capture the town. "Trains of cars from the North Carolina, the Wilmington & Weldon, the Raleigh & Gaston, and the Western N.C. Rail Roads, together with those belonging on the Atlantic Road, were run down to Newbern on the evening of the 28th," the *Union* reported. The militia arrived in the midst of snow and encamped on the green at New Bern Academy, making "a picturesque and romantic appearance, especially after lights had been put in them at night."

The next day opened with church bells ringing at dawn, accompanied by the booming calls of thirteen guns. Parades, maneuvers and the further booming of cannons went on throughout the day, and a special program was held on the academy green featuring Messieurs Hawks and Miller ("Eloquently and gracefully delivered," the *Union* proclaimed, "a splendid intellectual treat.") and instrumental music from bands.

When it had all ended, Oliver, diligent to his duties, auctioned off the granite plates to recoup their costs.

The Atlantic & North Carolina ran on ninety-five miles of track. If one boarded the train in Morehead City at 6:50 a.m., he could be in Goldsboro by 12:05 p.m.—a five-hour trip, with additional stops at four other stations. The official timetable at the start of 1861 was as follows:

Leave		*Arrive at*	
Morehead City	*6:50 a.m.*	*Carolina City*	*7 a.m.*
Carolina City	*7:05*	*New Bern*	*8:40*
New Bern	*9:10*	*Kinston*	*10:45*
Kinston	*10:55*	*Goldsboro*	*12:05*

Returning:

Goldsboro	*3:10 p.m.*	*Mosely Hall*	*3:45 p.m.*
Mosely Hall	*3:50*	*Kinston*	*4:20*
Kinston	*4:30*	*New Bern*	*6:05*
New Bern	*6:35*	*Carolina City*	*8:15*
Carolina City	*8:20*	*Morehead City*	*8:30*

In less than four and a half years, the Atlantic & North Carolina, from Morehead City to New Bern, would be in hostile, Yankee hands.

Let There Be Light

New ages are usually recognized after the fact. Wordsworth did not bump into Coleridge and shout, "Eureka! Did you feel that? Romanticism has begun!" No, they had tea, waxed eloquent over farm girls, ancient urns and lime tree bowers and then went off to play whist. They had no idea that they'd begun a major literary movement. But once in a while, a new age arrives in so tangible a form that you know it's occurred. Such was the case on September 15, 1859, when Ed Stanly (who lived in that funky house at 502 Pollock Street) gave the order to open the gas valves, flooding homes and businesses across the town with cheery light.

The New Bern Gas Company as it appeared in a publication in 1914. Curiously, the first seller of gas fixtures to the town was a music store. *From* Illustrated City of New Bern, *New Bern–Craven County Public Library.*

Preparations had been going on for weeks. Workers had been digging in the streets, laying pipes under the watchful eye of a Yankee gas specialist (H.J. Kirk) hired by Stanly's Newbern Gas Works. Throughout the summer, they had been plumbing the walls of prominent homes to snake the copper lines from room to room, while residents shopped a "splendid assortment" of "Plain and Ornamental Fixtures" provided by Alex Miller and Son (which also did the contract work of piping homes), sold at the rear of Hanff's Music Store. Gaslights were mounted on Pollock, South Front, East Front, Craven, Middle, Broad and Hancock Streets.

John L. Pennington's *Daily Progress* reported that the local militia companies held a military parade and "shook the very foundations of the great deep—Neuse and Trent—by their loud cannonading" ("great deep" in those days was apparently about ten feet, since the Neuse doesn't average a whole lot deeper).

You have to remember that before this event, illumination came in the form of bees' wax and tallow candles. Have you ever lit your home with nothing but candles? Have you tried to read by that pitiful, flickering light? Some of the most voracious readers of history went nearly blind doing that. Samuel Johnson was known, upon occasion, to set his wig on fire as he bent low over candles to see the page. No wonder people just gave it up at nine o'clock and went to bed.

Pennington gloried in the thought that, now, thirteen burners would turn his composing room into "a perfect flood of light" for the midnight printing sessions—no more "fretting and sweating" over candles. "What would the ghosts of our old fogy grandfathers have said could they have arisen last night and have taken a position on Hancock street and have seen the iron horse with his long train of elegant coaches move through the town by gas light and cross the Trent on the noble viaduct which spans it at the foot of the street?" he wondered in an editorial.

It made for a glorious couple of years before the darkness of the Civil War.

Part III

New Bern and the Civil War

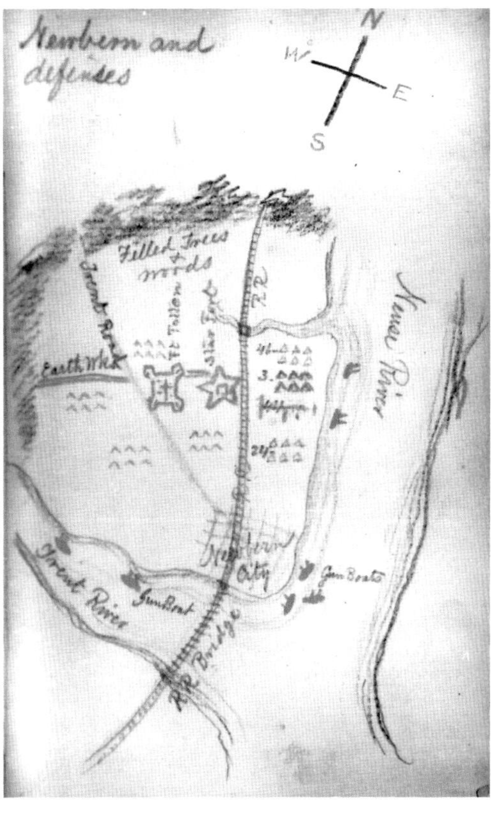

A drawing of the defenses of New Bern by Fred W. Smith, a soldier with the Forty-fourth Massachusetts. *Courtesy Tryon Palace Historic Sites and Gardens, New Bern, North Carolina.*

IF A FORT FALLS IN CHARLESTON, WILL IT MAKE A NOISE IN NEW BERN?

I had always heard and accepted the notion that New Bern was strongly pro-Union before the Civil War. But I've been digging through the *Newbern Daily Progress* of 1861, and I'm darned (sorry I couldn't say it stronger, Rhett) if I can find much evidence of Union sentiment in there.

One must read newspapers with a grain of salt, especially in a day when much of the news reported was learned from travelers on trains and when (just like today) convenient facts were often colored and tinted by the intentional omission of inconvenient ones. Misinformation was often king, and rumors regularly got reported as solid truths long before they could be verified.

North Carolina was the last state to actually secede, and it took two attempts to do that. An initial election was held on February 28, 1861, to determine whether the citizens even *wanted* to hold a secession convention. Statewide it failed, but New Bernians favored it by a margin of almost two to one. (The state actually seceded on May 20, by the way, and a New Bern representative, John D. Whitford, headed the committee that designed the newly Confederate state's flag.)

The bombing of Fort Sumter as seen from Fort Moultrie. Lithograph by Currier and Ives. *Courtesy Library of Congress, LC-USZ62-1652.*

New Bern's Union railroad station as it appeared in the late 1800s. Before the telegraph came to town, important news—including the fall of Fort Sumter—was often learned here first. *Courtesy John A. Clark Jr. Collection (#427), Special Collections Department, J.Y. Joyner Library, East Carolina University, Greenville, North Carolina.*

I will assume that you know that the Civil War began when soldiers in Charleston, South Carolina, opened fire on the Union-held Fort Sumter. Without a telegraph of their own, New Bernians had to wait for news of the event from a special train sent to Goldsboro. New Bern's sentiments regarding the Union were evident with the news of Fort Sumter's fall on April 13, 1861. The *Progress* reported:

> *Great excitement prevailed.*
>
> *The extra train got in between 9 and 10 o'clock Sunday night and was met by a hundred or two men who received the news with shouts of applause!*
>
> *At 10 o'clock, seven guns were fired in honor of the seven Confederate States and bonfires sent up a brilliant volume of smoke and flame.—Soon thereafter, "The Father of the Faithful"* [Lincoln] *was hung in effigy on top of the ruins of the old court house* [it had burned down a couple of months before].
>
> *We passed yesterday morning about 10 o'clock and he was still dangling in the air with a pasteboard upon his brow, in large letters, was the following*

> *inscription, "May all Abolitionists meet the same fate." About a dozen little boys were busy pelting him with stones.*

The Elm City Rifles—a local militia that would fight nobly throughout the war as part of the Second North Carolina Regiment—held an impromptu parade, with New Bern belles smiling and waving handkerchiefs from their doors and windows.

Up in Washington, D.C., Lincoln was reacting, too. After all, he had allowed the whole Fort Sumter crisis to simmer and boil in the hopes that he could get the South to fire the first shot and take the blame for starting the war. On April 15, he made his famous—or infamous—call for seventy-five thousand troops to quell the rebellion. North Carolina, up to that time uncommitted, and New Bern, a town that had apparently been on a fire-eating diet for some months, responded quickly. Just not in the way Lincoln had hoped.

North Carolina's governor, John W. Ellis, who'd been secretly preparing the state for war all along, wrote a famous response to Simon Cameron, Lincoln's secretary of war, on the same day:

> *RALEIGH, April 15, 1861. HON. SIMON CAMERON, Secretary of War;*
>
> *Your dispatch is received, and, if genuine, which its extraordinary character leads me to doubt, I have to say in reply that I regard the levy of troops made by the Administration for the purpose of subjugating the States of the South, as in violation of the Constitution and a usurpation of power. I can be no party to this wicked violation of the laws of the country, and to this war upon the liberties of a free people. You can get no troops from North Carolina. I will reply more in detail when your call is received by mail.*
>
> *—John W. Ellis, Governor of North Carolina*

Two days later, Ellis issued his own call for troops. One could argue that secession was a technicality—it was really on that day, April 17, 1861, when North Carolina entered the Civil War.

Anniversary dates are always hard to pin down in North Carolina, because Tarheels just can't make up their minds about anything in one day. Voters had vetoed the bill to consider secession on February 28, but Sumter (April 13), Lincoln (April 15) and Ellis (April 17) had all worked to turn even the most ardent Unionist into a Rebel with a cause. Dissolution was, for all practical purposes, a done deal almost before April was halfway over.

Burned to ruins in a fire on January 15, 1861, the Craven County Courthouse on Middle Street became a site of anti-Union protest with the hanging of Lincoln in effigy two months later. *Courtesy North Carolina Office of Archives and History, Raleigh, North Carolina.*

New Bern sent numerous men to the war; a stroll through Cedar Grove Cemetery will bring you to several veterans' grave sites, along with the Confederate monument to the Battle of New Bern's dead. Several New Bern militia companies besides the Elm City Rifles—such as the Beauregard Rifles—helped fill the ranks of several regiments.

North Carolina was the Confederacy's breadbasket, as well as its main supply depot, source of clothing and provider of men and blood. With a white population of 631,000, North Carolina mustered some 125,000 soldiers for the war, significantly more than any other state. Its casualties were also far greater: 20,602, more than any of its Southern sisters.

The first official Southern casualty of the war was North Carolinian Henry Wyatt at the Battle of Bethel on June 10, 1861. The highest casualty rate of any regiment was the Twenty-sixth North Carolina: 714 of its 800 men, at Gettysburg. On roll call the second day of the battle, Company G only had one man to answer, and the sergeant gave roll call from a stretcher.

Ours were the first regiments in battle (Bethel), penetrated most deeply into enemy lines at Gettysburg and Chickamauga, fired the last salvo before

Lee's surrender at Appomattox and were the last to disband after Lee's surrender. Our sons of the Confederacy can be proud.

Gabriel Rains's Bloody Invention

A childhood resident of New Bern, Gabriel Rains pursued a gruesome fascination that resulted in one of the world's most hated weapons.

It was May 4, 1862, when (by proxy) a Yankee horse rider made Gabriel Rains's acquaintance. It must have been emotional for him, because he went all to pieces. Literally.

Gabriel Rains is one of those men we claim by association. He didn't live in New Bern as an adult, but he was a child here and his family was well known. From what we can tell, his father was a real hoot.

Gabriel would make his mark, for good or ill, in the Civil War. So, in fact, would his younger brother, George. The boys (two of eight siblings) were fond of explosives, and while Gabriel was inventing some fearsome weapons, his brother was successfully heading up the effort to keep an armaments-poor Confederacy in gunpowder during five years of war.

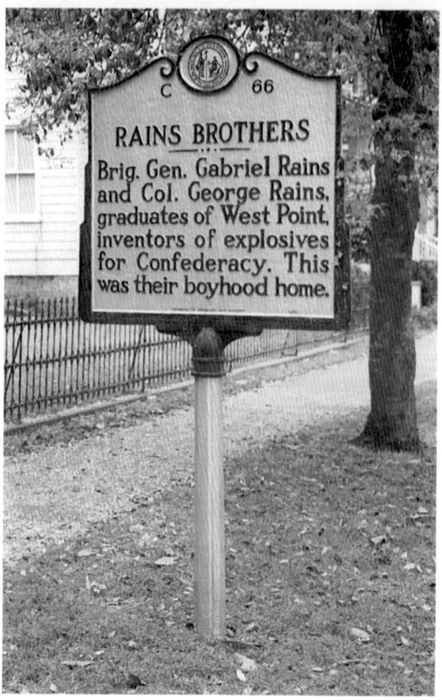

A historic marker in front of the Rains house describes the history of its most famous childhood inhabitants. *Photo by the author.*

The Rains house stands at 605 East Front Street, though it was moved there from Johnson Street some years ago, and it has been so altered that Gabriel would probably have a hard time recognizing it. The whole family who squeezed inside it made for a curious lot. The father, Gabriel Manigault Rains, was a respected cabinetmaker. One son, John, graduated from Chapel Hill College in 1823 and had a successful career as a lawyer. He was bitten by the acting bug and was cited, by onetime resident Stephen F. Miller, as having been as "admirable as

'Caleb Quotem,'" a popular stock character from the 1808 play *Wags of Windsor* by George Coleman.

Gabriel and George, however, found their pleasure in the theatrics of chemicals and explosions. "George is certainly one of the best of sons," Miller quoted his mother as saying, "but I can't keep the boy decent; he burns up with his 'chemicals,' as he calls them, the best clothing I can have made for him. I never feel sure that he has a single suit not in holes."

Gabriel was about as bad. It only made sense that he wound up with a military career. He began to tinker with his most famous invention while serving in Florida.

In the 1830s and 1840s, Florida was a hotbed of Seminole insurrection. The federal government had demanded that the Seminoles pack their bags and head for reservations west of the Mississippi, but the majority of the tribe, led by their greatest warrior-chief, Osceola (who was part Irish, curiously enough), demurred. And so Fort King was built in 1827 in a wasteland that has turned into the little city of Ocala today. Fort King (named after military commander Colonel William King) was built on a small hill near the Ocklawaha River (Seminole, I'm going to guess, for "Try to say *this*, white man!"). It was one of those split-log structures, complete with a blockhouse, kitchens and quarters for officers and enlisted men. It served as a kind of way station between other, larger forts in the territory.

Gabriel Rains as a young officer, when he toyed with mines in Florida, from *The Photographic History of the Civil War in Ten Volumes*, volume 5, *Forts and Artillery* (1911).

Rains was assigned as a captain to Fort King. In 1840, faced with superior numbers of skillful foes, he started toying with the idea of land mines. It wasn't that Rains was afraid to come out and fight; he *did*, and with notable courage. But the Seminoles—who never *were* completely run out Florida—excelled at materializing, seemingly out of nowhere, firing their shots and melting back into the Florida forests. Rains decided to try an "out of nowhere" tactic of his own.

With a few of his men, he jury-rigged a live shell, hiding it under a blanket near a pond the natives were known to frequent. A Seminole set it off and several were killed. Encouraged by this success, Gabriel tried again. Returning, he discovered that this time his device had done no harm. On his way back to Fort King, he and his men were ambushed. They made it back, but he was so badly wounded that obituaries were sent to several newspapers. As a result of his service, Rains was brevetted a major on April 28, 1840.

When the Mexican-American War broke out in 1846, Rains was one of the first Americans to go. We know, of course, what a great training ground that war was for the generals who would maneuver and slay across the American landscape from 1861 to 1865. As in the Seminole War, he would become known for his occasionally reckless bravery.

When the Civil War came, the Rains brothers both signed on with the Confederate side. Neither would directly fight battles but instead would concentrate on supporting the troops through weapons supply. George worked his saltpeter magic in Georgia, while Gabriel handled weapons requisitions from Richmond. It was here where his Seminole experiences played on his mind. He began experimenting with pressure-activated fuses and tripwires. He got his chance to test his new device when he oversaw the retreat of Confederates from Yorktown in 1862.

On May 4, 1862, a rider, possibly scouting near the town, set the first one off. One source declared the fellow to have been a Yankee and another to have been a civilian. Toss your coin and choose your truth—such is history. A number of soldiers died from the mines over the next few days. The indignant Union brigadier general William F. Barry described it, from the *Official Records of the Rebellion*:

> *Several of our men were injured by the explosion of what was ascertained to be loaded shells buried…a few inches below the surface of the ground, and so arranged…that they exploded by being trod upon or otherwise disturbed. In some cases articles of common use, and which would be most likely to be picked up, such as engineers' wheelbarrows, or pickaxes, or shovels, were laid upon the spot with apparent carelessness. Concealed strings or wires leading from the friction primer of the shell to the superincumbent articles were so arranged that the slightest disturbance would occasion the explosion.*

Rains began to experiment with a new fuse for his mines the following winter; he would lose a thumb and forefinger to his work. Slowly, he developed a highly sensitive fuse that would continue to be used until 1983. According to a land mine awareness webpage, several of Rains's land mines were found in 1960 and were determined to still be quite potent.

Rains's invention lives on and is one of the most controversial weapons in use today. Twenty-four thousand people are maimed or killed by land mines every year—one every twenty-two minutes. Most victims are not soldiers.

Land mines were just as controversial in the Civil War. Here is General Barry again:

> *These shells were not thus placed on the glacis at the bottom of the ditch, &c., which, in view of an anticipated assault, might possibly be considered a legitimate use of them, but they were basely planted by an enemy who was secretly abandoning his post on common roads, at springs of water, in the shade of trees, at the foot of telegraph poles, and, lastly, quite within the defenses of the place—in the very streets of the town…I was myself a witness of the horrible mangling by one of these shells of a cavalryman and his horse outside of the main work upon the Williamsburg road, and also of the cruel murder in the very streets of Yorktown of an intelligent young telegraph operator, who, while in the act of approaching a telegraph pole to reconnect a broken wire, trod upon one of these shells villainously concealed at its foot. It is generally understood that these shells were prepared by General George W. Rains, of the Confederate Army, for his brother, Brig. Gen. Gabriel Rains, the commander of the post of Yorktown, at whose instigation they were prepared and planted. The belief of the complicity of General Gabriel Rains in this dastardly business is confirmed by the knowledge possessed by many others of our Army of a similar mode of warfare inaugurated by him while disgracing the uniform of the American Army during the Seminole War in Florida.*

Harsh words, strongly felt.

General Rains, a New Bern son, developed his gruesome devices as a desperate means of overcoming vastly superior numbers. Perhaps, in the grand scheme of things, the mines had no great military effect on the war—beyond the growing bitterness of Yankees who died by them and held guns on Confederate prisoners who were forced to dig them up and disarm them.

Still, one victim every twenty-two minutes is a legacy to think about.

COLONEL SINCLAIR DOESN'T EXACTLY SAVE THE DAY

Among the many things that went wrong for Confederate forces in the Battle of New Bern were the error-based expectations and the performance of this Union-leaning minister turned Confederate-soldier.

The Battle of New Bern featured a number of mistakes that cost the fight. Despite the city's (and state's) pleas, Richmond did not send troops sufficient to defend the town. The general in charge of the defenses (Lawrence O'Brian Branch), while intelligent and dedicated, was a politician with no military experience. The city, in laying river mines (called "torpedoes" then) and having "Yankee catchers" in the river to trip up gunboats, sent slaves to do the labor, and when the Yankees arrived, the slaves went out and showed them where the obstacles lay.

During the battle, the most vital position in the Confederate line was manned by a militia company that had only been together for a couple of weeks, men who were armed with anything from shotguns to squirrel guns and, who knows, maybe even popguns. A large cannon, which would have added a powerful defense to the weak break in the Confederate line along a railroad track, was not brought in time to use.

Here's another bit of bad mojo that worked into the defeat of the Confederates. A particular officer's actions, if performed differently the day before the battle, might have helped bring about a very different outcome in the fight. Take Colonel—*Reverend* Colonel—James Sinclair.

A Presbyterian minister in civilian life, Sinclair was a bit of an anomaly in New Bern in 1862: a Confederate who'd actually experienced a battle. Originally a chaplain with the Fifth North Carolina, he'd seen action at Manassas (First Bull Run) the previous July. This "fighting chaplain," the story went, had led the men of the Fifth in several advances on that bloody field. General James Longstreet was so impressed after the fight that he offered him a position in his command. Ask anyone.

When he signed on to the Thirty-fifth North Carolina, the tale of his heroics circulated throughout the regiment, and his fellow officers voted him colonel in command. It seemed an obvious choice.

General Branch was thankful to have him. He had a few good, trained soldiers under him, such as future heroes Henry Burgwyn and Robert F. Hoke. But even those men had yet to "see the elephant" (fight a battle).

A few miles below the line of the current New Bern battlefield (two or three miles of breastworks going inland from the earthen Fort Thompson by the river) was a powerful line called the Croatan Breastworks. Branch believed that he could hold that line against all comers with just two thousand men and a couple of cannons. But behind the line was six miles of riverfront that could not be easily defended. Yankees could land anywhere along here and take the Croatan line from behind. To compensate, Branch dug rifle pits above and below the line. Rising on the ridge twenty-five feet above the river, he felt that he could make any attempted landing very costly. He ordered Sinclair and his men to man the pits. Reinforcements, he promised, would soon be sent.

General Branch must have pinned a lot of hopes on his fighting reverend—Sinclair's orders were to open fire on any attempted landing by Yankees and to protect the flanks of two well-drilled, though inexperienced, regiments (the Seventh and Twenty-sixth) that were manning the vital Croatan Breastworks near the expected landing site. Eventually, he most likely would have to pull back—the enemy was bound to land upstream and attempt to flank him. But still, the three regiments could buy time for the main line and exact a dear price from the enemy. Trains were waiting to hurry them back to the Fort Thompson line.

General Branch and Sinclair's men felt secure in their leader's experience and bravery. But here was the fatal flaw: Sinclair's story of Bull Run heroism turned out to be more bull than run, and his loyalty to the Confederate cause was highly negligible if not outright treasonous. The battle's failure—rather than its hopes—would lie to some extent with him.

Sinclair listened to the voices of his enemy on their boats the night of March 13, and it must have spooked him. When some Union gunboats started firing on the pits, instead of ordering his men to "hunker down," he called for retreat. No men were lost in the shelling, though one was killed and two wounded in the retreat. The reinforcements arrived about this time and, finding the rifle pits abandoned, knew that it would be impossible to hold the Croatan line. With no one protecting their flanks, the Seventh and the Twenty-sixth had no choice but to retreat as well. Thus, much to the later astonishment of the Yankees, the city's strongest fortifications were not manned.

Sinclair's men were now with the main force holding the Fort Thompson line, a line you can still see along the west side of the Craven County Fairgrounds along Highway 70 today. They were placed near the inexperienced militia—a small army of citizens that had been recruited from town just two weeks earlier and that was manning, bizarrely enough, the weakest point of the Confederate line, along the railroad tracks. Here, where an old brick kiln stood, the front line jumped back several hundred yards up the river, behind a heavy swamp. The unnatural angle thus created

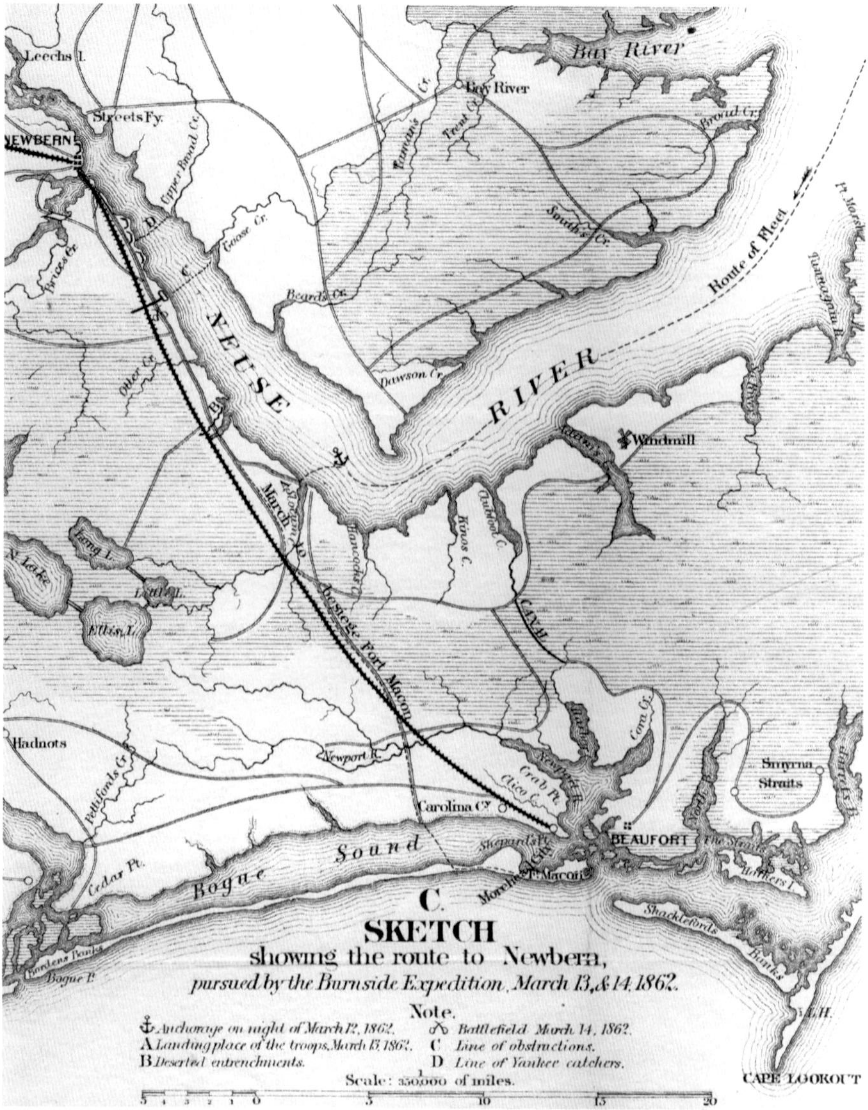

This map shows the route of General Burnside's forces in their March attack on New Bern. The "deserted entrenchments," B, are those from which Colonel Sinclair withdrew. *From the personal collection of the author.*

was exposed and was easy prey for any enemy fortunate enough to realize it. It was at this position that an extra cannon was hauled up at the last minute to plug up the hole, but the shooting match started before it could be wrestled into place.

Early in the battle, Sinclair's men saw a wondrous sight. The Union general Jesse Reno suddenly appeared, standing within easy shot, talking with his officers. The soldiers wanted to pick him off, but Sinclair would not allow it, declaring such an act ungentlemanly. A couple of hours into the fight, the Union forces flanked the militia at the railroad, routing them. Rather than taking up the slack, some of the men of the Thirty-fifth joined the militiamen in their flight. Sinclair briefly attempted to keep the rest at the line and then gave it up and sent up his second order of retreat. With his regiment's withdrawal, the rest of Branch's army was exposed, and the battle was essentially lost. The victorious Yankees would be feasting for dinner on meals left behind by fleeing New Bern citizens.

Let's conclude with "the rest of the story." General Branch must have been greatly disappointed in the man who'd come so highly recommended. We know that Sinclair's men were: they blamed their flight on the preacher and voted him out of his colonelcy within days. Perhaps their blame was well placed, as the regiment would fight bravely in the future.

Sinclair had gained his position in part because of his perceived heroism at Manassas, a heroism that received strong kudos, it was believed, from General Longstreet himself. But this story turned out to be an extreme exaggeration. While he *was* commended after the battle for acting as a field officer and "render[ing] me all the assistance in his power" by the Fifth's lieutenant colonel, J.P. Jones, there is no record of him being commended by Longstreet. Besides, as Jones wrote in the same report, the Fifth had done nothing more at Manassas than a bit of skirmishing.

The members of Thirty-fifth, in its biography, noted the falsity of the story and their disgust with Sinclair. Newspapers were no kinder, calling him a coward and a traitor. It was not long before he resigned from the Confederate services.

Sinclair was at heart a Unionist. Born in Scotland and trained in Pennsylvania, he was a Presbyterian minister who had preached a sermon that his congregation found too abolitionist. His parishioners were so disturbed that they threatened to lynch him. Relatives advised him to join the Confederate army to protect his family. He testified to Congress after the war that he had never really wanted to fight for the South. "Have you ever willingly done any act to promote the rebellion?" he was asked at this hearing. His answer: "Not willingly."

One historian declared that Sinclair went so far as to sign on as chaplain for a Union regiment before the war ended and called him "a notorious figure in the Reconstruction."

The Chaplain and the King's Communion Set

One of the finest Southern chaplains—who hid Christ Church's most valuable treasure from Yankee vandals—was himself a Yankee native.

While Reverend Sinclair proved to be a great disappointment in the Civil War, there were other men of the cloth who proved much more honorable. Among them was Reverend Dr. Alfred Augustin Watson, who couldn't help but become a strong and virtuous man dragging around such a name.

A Brooklyn native, he had taken his first orders with a Plymouth, North Carolina church in 1844. Twice he was asked to take the reins at Christ Church, and twice he refused, before finally accepting in 1858. Local historian Gertrude Carraway declared that he rapidly became "[o]ne of the most beloved of all local and East Carolina churchmen." Over the years, he would show such value and discernment that, in 1884, he became the first bishop of the Eastern North Carolina Diocese of the Episcopal Church.

When war broke out, New Bern's men turned out in multitudes to form a number of companies to fill the regimental ranks. Three local militias helped to form the Second North Carolina, and Reverend Watson signed on

Reverend Alfred Watson. *Courtesy Christ Episcopal Church Archives, New Bern.*

as regimental chaplain. The congregation asked him to keep his rectorate, and so he remained on the vestry's books until the town's fall. Reverend William Wetmore (sounds just like a name you'd give a sitcom sidekick, doesn't it?) was hired in September 1861 to keep the home church running while Reverend Watson was off at war.

Christ Church as it appears today. *Photo by the author.*

Watson did more than tend to the soldiers' spiritual needs—he also watched the enemy's movements. "His information of the topography of the country was of great value to our commanding officer," Captain Matthew Manly of Company D remembered of his chaplain's scouting work. "He had the profound respect of every man."

Watson could not return to New Bern after its fall, though Wetmore hung in for another year. Union chaplains were placed in charge of services, which was a better fate for Christ Church than some other churches received. First Baptist became a warehouse of sorts, while First Presbyterian was a hospital with a "dead house" assembled on the grounds.

Midway through the war, Watson became rector of St. Paul's in Wilmington, where he remained for some years.

Christ's Church maintains a valuable communion service donated by King George in 1752. A popular story tells how Reverend Watson spirited it out of town, carrying it to Wilmington for safekeeping. Later, Reverend Hoke watched over it in Fayetteville, hiding it amid old rubbish in a closet. Yankees entered the town, searching for loot, and dug through the closet. Seeing all the rubbish, they looked no further and so, through this simple

The communion set of King George II. *Photo by the author.*

ruse, missed a most valuable prize. While Ms. Carraway did not mention this event in her fine church history, a 1922 booklet about the church does. It certainly seems within his character. True or not, the legend reflects the real character and style of this interesting man.

CONTRABAND IN NEW BERN

If you look up the name "Vincent Colyer" on the Internet, you will discover a New York painter who made his greatest fame as an artist of the American West. He was an activist for the rights of Native Americans when such activism was hardly a popular thing (1868–71). You can find a number of his ethereal, panoramic paintings and intricate sketches with a simple Google search. What you may not find as easily is his contributions to New Bern during the Civil War.

Colyer entered the war as a civilian representing the Christian Commission in New York. He signed on to Burnside's massive train of ships and gained the general's notice through his dedicated work among the sick and wounded soldiers, as well as through his duties under the regimental chaplains. Once in New Bern, the general was quickly overcome by the sight of slaves celebrating and thanking the men in blue for their freedom. The numbers of black families multiplied rapidly, and Burnside soon discovered that adequately overseeing this influx of "contraband" was more than his officers could handle. Also, there was the condition of the poor whites who had not fled with their wealthier

Vincent Colyer penned numerous illustrations of the lives of newly freed blacks in New Bern in his *Report of the Services Rendered by the Freed People to the United States Army in North Carolina.*

fellow citizens—some whites made poorer, no doubt, by the marauding patrols of Yankee soldiers.

He turned to Colyer, a devout Christian, whose heart was obviously strong for the blacks, and on March 31, 1862, he named him superintendent of the poor for the North Carolina department.

Along with his duties of seeing to the food and sheltering of poor blacks and whites, Colyer was also given the responsibility of recruiting the former slaves to work building docks and forts in New Bern and along the chain of barrier islands now under Union control.

Colyer quickly became an admirer of the black race. Whereas numerous Yankees took advantage of the new freedmen as cheap laborers and complained of and ridiculed them in letters sent home, Colyer saw a people desperate to gain an education and make an honest living. He oversaw the development of schools and churches during his administration. He hired several thousand to work on the forts at a rate of eight dollars per month plus a suit of clothes (not that much less than a soldier's wages). "In the four months that I had charge of them," he wrote in his booklet, *Report of the Services Rendered By the Freed People to the United States Army, in North Carolina in 1864*, "the men built three first-class earthwork forts: Fort Totten, at Newbern—a large work; Fort Burnside, on the upper end of Roanoke Island; and Fort _____, at Washington, N.C. These three forts were our chief reliance for defence against the rebels."

Colyer soon discovered another valuable use for the freedmen under his charge: as spies for the Union. They proved to be quick-witted observers who knew the enemy's territory and could travel with relative ease through Confederate country. His report included the adventures of several such men. Furney Bryant was one of his favorites. "At that time now two years ago, he did not know a letter of the alphabet, and he came within our lines dressed in the rags of the plantation," Colyer recalled. Bryant worked hard to earn Colyer's and the other Union men's trust, running dangerous spying missions and attending the schools to learn how to read and write.

In *Report of the Services Rendered*, Colyer described the mission of a former slave named Charley who made three trips to spy out Confederate headquarters in Kinston:

> *The distance was forty-five miles, thirty within the enemy's lines. On the first visit, he brought us information that the enemy's camp and a large portion of his forces were removed some miles and across a river. Upon the closest questioning by the General, no discrepancy or contradiction could be found in his statements. On his third journey, in company with another boy, he was about five miles above Kingston, when he was suddenly overtaken by a rebel on horseback, with a pack of bloodhounds by his side, scouring the woods, and the dogs evidently on their trail. The negroes waited cautiously in a thick copse of wood, and as the man rode round the thicket, before the dogs came up, they fired their revolvers at him. They missed the man but shot his horse. In a minute the dogs came in, when they turned quickly and shot two of the dogs. The man hearing the repeated firing and the howling of his dogs, and unable to tell the character or numbers of his enemies, quickly ran off. The boys also ran in the opposite direction with equal, or perhaps, superior alertness, for they had farther to go to reach home—some thirty-six miles to our nearest pickets. They continued to run and rest at intervals, until they were within twelve miles of our lines, when they heard the bark of more dogs, and the sound of men's voices urged them on. Knowing that the dogs were after them, and realizing their danger, they ran very fast, and taking to the water in the swamps, whenever possible, for several miles they baffled the scent of the dogs, and kept at a distance ahead of them. At last, seeing that they were nearly upon them, and the men a long distance behind, they quickly got ready their revolvers, and awaited the attack of the dogs. Placing their backs against trees, they took cool and deliberate aim, and wounded three of them, and sent them howling back to their owners. The men in pursuit, hearing the firing and howling of the dogs, set up a shout and hurried forward, until they came near the place where the fight had occurred, when they advanced, it is supposed, more cautiously, fearing an ambush. The negro boys came home as fast as they could run, throwing off coats, pants, caps, and everything but their shirts, drawers, and revolvers, finally reaching our lines in safety, completely exhausted.*

A free school for newly freed slaves helped many but was controversial in a state whose prewar laws had outlawed the education of blacks. From Vincent Colyer's 1864 *Report of the Services Rendered.*

Not everyone favored Colyer's schools—or even the freeing of slaves in the community. Edward Stanly, son of the congressman and duelist John Stanly, had been named military governor over North Carolina by Abraham Lincoln. It was a dearly held Yankee belief that North Carolina was full of Unionists who would flock to the cause if only the right man took the governor's seat. Stanly had the reputation of family as well as strong Union sympathies. Called out of California, he settled into his old town but quickly let the president know that he meant to obey North Carolina law and, therefore, had no desire to aid the colored cause. He and Colyer soon got into an argument over the schools, the governor citing state legislation that outlawed education for blacks. He resigned his post in January 1863 after Lincoln issued the Emancipation Proclamation. The North learned that Union sympathizers were not nearly so rabid for the cause as had been hoped, while Stanly gained himself a reputation as a traitor to his home state for years to come.

In the summer of 1863, New Bern began recruiting for colored regiments within North Carolina. Commanding major general John G. Foster was not fond of the idea, but he did nothing to inhibit Brigadier General Edward Augustus Wild, a Massachusetts homeopathic doctor who was put in charge of building four such regiments.

Wild recruited the half brother of Harriet Beecher Stowe to serve as colonel over the First North Carolina Colored Volunteers. This was

James Beecher, youngest brother of the world-famous preacher Henry Ward Beecher.

Beecher was a preacher himself who had spent five years as a missionary to China. He was not known for his stable mind: he'd recently been discharged as chaplain of the 141st New York Regiment, which he had helped recruit, to recover from a bout of madness at a sanitarium. But Wild saw him as a reliable and capable man who was a fervent abolitionist and brought him on board. Furney Bryant would be among the first volunteers to sign on as a soldier.

Beecher was impressed by his colored troops. In a letter to a woman named Frances Perkins, he boasted:

> *I am amazed at the promptitude of these men to learn military drill and in less than three weeks I shall have a battalion which any man might be proud of. There is an amount of muscle which no regiment in the service can boast of…I wish doubtful people at home could see my three week's regiment. They would talk less nonsense about negro inferiority.*

Trained, the regiment would serve alongside the more famous Fifty-fourth Massachusetts in South Carolina. Though set, at first, to heavy manual labor, the men eventually got their chance at battle and distinguished themselves in Olustee, Florida. Furney Bryant quickly rose to the position of first sergeant (colored troops were not allowed to hold commissioned officers' posts).

Vincent Colyer had long moved back to his work in New York City when, in 1864, he was surprised by a visit from Bryant, who was on leave. Colyer was impressed in the changes from the ragged, ill-educated slave who had come to him in New Bern a year or so before. "The contrast in his personal appearance, in his new suit of Army blue, was not more remarkable than the…letter [I] received from him since his return to duty…Let no one say that freedom is not better than slavery, with such examples before them," he wrote.

Bryant then returned to visit New Bern, where he and his comrades who were on leave with him arrived "in time to participate in the defence of that place against the recent desperate attack of the rebels in February, 1864," Colyer concluded.

Henry James's Brother and the Fifty-fourth Massachusetts

If you have had the pleasure of advanced American literature classes, you have no doubt read *Daisy Miller* or *The Turn of the Screw* by Henry James. And if you are a fan of war movies, you've probably seen the 1989 film *Glory*, the story of the first colored regiment in the North (the Fifty-fourth Massachusetts) and its epic and tragic charge of Charleston's Fort Wagner. It turns out that both Mr. James and the Fifty-fourth had some ties to wartime New Bern.

The Fifty-fourth, formed in 1863, was officered by Robert Gould Shaw, a young and wealthy son of Boston abolitionists. Shaw, a Harvard man, was obligated to fill up his officer corps with whites. Naturally, he wanted men with experience, as well as men who shared his abolitionist views. Perhaps he and Massachusetts governor John Andrew consulted before Andrew decided to seek these officers from a regiment that was already in the field.

That regiment was the Forty-fourth Massachusetts, a nine-months unit that served its entire term in and around the captured city of New Bern. It was a company of wealthy young men, a few of them abolitionists and many of them Harvard students looking for heroic adventure and possibly a scar to show the girls back home. Colonel Francis L. Lee, the commanding officer, received a letter on February 18, 1863, seeking potential officers. He passed it to his men and several responded. A few would pay with their lives at the Battles of Fort Wagner and Honey Hill.

Most of the candidates came from the regiment's elite Company F—Sergeant Cabot Russel was one and William Simpkins, a private, another. Then there was their friend, Sergeant Garth "Wilkie" James. He was the son of Henry James Sr., promoter of a theology known as Swedenborgianism. Wilkie's brother was Henry James Jr., who would ultimately leave America to live in Europe and write his novels that—as Woody Allen once wrote of the classics—"We all love and avoid."

Wilkie, who was only seventeen when he signed up, was no Sunday abolitionist. He believed that "slavery was a monstrous wrong, its destruction worthy of a man's best effort, even unto the laying down of his life."

The chosen men were mustered out of their regiment and shipped to Readville, Massachusetts, where they set about training the experimental army of blacks. It must have been a bit of an old-home day for them, for this was the very camp where the Forty-fourth had learned to drill.

Wilkie, his pals Cabot and William and the other officers formerly of the Forty-fourth marched at the fore of their regiment when it left Boston

One of the batteries that took part in siege operations before the advance of the Fifty-fourth Massachusetts black regiment in 1863. *Courtesy Library of Congress, LC-DIG-cwpb-04741.*

on May 28, 1863. The Fifty-fourth found itself doing manual labor for some time but finally saw action on James Island, South Carolina, on July 16. They carried themselves well, won the fight and paid a price of forty-two casualties.

Two days later, they marched into history in the ill-fated assault on Battery Wagner, a well-armed fort guarding the approaches to Charleston. If you have seen the movie, you know the ultimate result; if you have not, then by all means rent it.

Russel and Simpkins would be among the enormous casualties in the assault, dying near Colonel Shaw. Wilkie would survive, but only just. He once described his part in the fight to a fellow officer: "When we received the first discharge of the enemy's cannon [I gathered] together a knot of men after the suspense of a few seconds, I waved my sword for a further charge towards the living line of fire above us. We had gone then some thirty yards, but determinedly onwards, the ranks obliquely following the swords of those they trusted." He was wounded in the side by a shell but kept going. Then a canister ball hit his foot, an injury that put him out of the action. He dragged himself some distance until he was found and rescued. After the battle, he returned home to recuperate.

Wilkie's injury was bad enough that he resigned in July 1864, but his heart was big enough that he found a way back into the Fifty-fourth at the end of the year. The wound would continue harassing him the rest of his life.

The End of the *Underwriter*

The Confederates would never win New Bern back, but they did manage one fine moral victory.

They called Captain Jacob Westervelt's ship the *Underwriter*, but after the Confederacy got through with it, the name *Underwater* would have been more appropriate, or maybe the *All-over-the-water*.

It was a Federal gunboat, a side-wheel steamer anchored at New Bern in defense of the Union-held town. Occasionally it forayed down the Neuse and up the sounds, making itself a nuisance to its Confederate foes.

After New Bern fell, the city's blue-coated captors lost no time in turning the place into a heavily armed camp. Soldiers arrived by the thousands, gunboats plied the waters and earthwork forts appeared like mounds built by mutant prairie dogs. One, Fort Totten, was especially lethal, composed of steep earthen walls behind which scowling soldiers and very big guns lay waiting. Today it is an innocuous playground, its last earthworks having been bulldozed for construction projects some years ago.

By 1864, the town was well entrenched. Still, the Confederacy dreamed that New Bern's store of supplies would look mighty fine in the Stars and Bars commissary. Robert E. Lee, hoping that the town might be a little too sure of itself, suggested to President Jeff Davis that, perhaps, New Bern was ripe for a fall. Jeff concurred.

John Taylor Wood. *Courtesy U.S. Naval Historical Center.*

A land battle could not be won, however, so long as the Yankees were covered by gunboats. The *Underwriter* needed to be put out of commission—or, better yet, put into *Confederate* commission. It would take a daring band to capture a ship from the very jaws of a Union stronghold. Jeff knew just the man to lead it: his nephew, John Taylor Wood.

Wood was known for bold raids on Union shipping—he'd burned his share of boats and had commanded the privateer *Tallahassee*, destroyer of twenty-six Union vessels in its brief career.

Wood's plan was simple if risky. Several small boats with a dozen men each would row the fifty or so miles down the Neuse from Kinston to a point across the river from where the *Underwriter* was moored; then they would turn and attack it in the early hours of February 2. The men would storm the craft, boarding it with small arms and using the element of surprise to overrun the crew and capture the boat. Then they would stoke the engines and turn the ship against its former owners.

To Wood's advantage, only two other boats were guarding the town that night—"inferior boats," in the words of Union brigadier general I.N. Palmer—the *Commodore Hull* and the *Lockwood*. To Wood's disadvantage was the fact that the gunboat they wanted was moored near three strong Union forts.

Confederate naval surgeon Daniel Conrad was among the sailors chosen for the mission. Ten boats and 120 men would take part, "every one of whom were young, vigorous, fully alive and keen for the prospective work," the surgeon recalled twenty-five years later.

They embarked down the Neuse River from Kinston on Sunday, February 1. At sundown they encamped on an island sixty miles from their target, and "in distinct and terse terms," Commander Wood gave the volunteers their instructions. Dr. Conrad recalled that Commander Wood "thereupon…offered up the most touching appeal to the Almighty that it has ever been my fortune to have heard…it was the last ever heard by many a poor fellow and deeply felt by every one."

They sailed under cover of night. Among those sailors was at least one New Bernian, Captain David Sermonds, who had a post of some honor—pilot on Commander Wood's own boat—according to Colonel John Whitford, a New Bern historian who had been an administrative officer in the war.

The soldiers passed two points where Union pickets were suspected and sat on their oars, drifting in silence, undiscovered. At about 3:30 in the morning, they arrived in New Bern and hunted cautiously for their prey, using the city's lights to guide them. Though they searched, even daring to approach close to some wharves, "Not a gunboat could be seen," Dr. Conrad said. "None was there." Eventually, the rising sun joined the Union cause, forcing the saboteurs to seek shelter on an upstream island to wait out the day.

During that day, help came from unexpected quarters—both Confederate and Yankee. In the occupied town, Brigadier General Palmer advised that the *Underwriter* be moved to "an advanced position in the Upper Neuse" (his report is cited in the *War of the Rebellion* official records). This placed the boat in easy reach, about five miles from the island, although still within protective range of Union forts on land. Captain Westervelt carried out these orders, the last he would receive in this world.

The Confederate sailors watched with happy amazement as the side-wheel gunboat steamed into view about sundown. Soon after, a large launch with fifteen men and a howitzer appeared as additional aid to the Confederate cause. At about 9:00 p.m., the sailors started their final approach toward their prey.

The launches pulled slowly and cautiously down the river toward town. Commander Wood sat in his boat, watching the floating bulk that was his target grow slowly closer in the dark. With him was his coxswain, Captain David Hassell, who had served with him on the *Tallahassee.*

It would take them four hours to row the five miles to the east side of the river opposite the *Underwriter*. There they angled their boats for the ride across, hoping that they would reach its side without being found out.

Whitford described the raid as told to him by Hassell:

> *Finally opposite the enemy's vessel the turn is made and the command "pull for the ship boys and your life" rings out. In a moment the Underwriter's sides are all aflame in the dark night, and the water shake and the air roar*

The attack on the USS *Underwriter*, from an 1863 *Frank Leslie's Illustrated Newspaper* edition.

with her guns. Captain Wood looks back: "Steady, steady!" and "Pull, boys, pull!" are his only words. The dead and dying in the boat are not heeded. One lies between the coxswain's feet, yet the helm is held with unflinching grasp. On, on, the boats rush. Another volley and more dead and wounded.

Daniel Conrad had bloody tales to tell of the craft's boarding. His own boat was slated to open the action, but its coxswain was shot dead, a bullet in his head. Another boat under Lieutenant Loyall touched the *Underwriter* first, and its men piled on. Loyall, being nearsighted, tripped and fell on the deck; the four men following behind him were shot dead by the defending crew. Dr. Conrad found the deck slick with blood. He was led by a comrade to assist a wounded youth whose head, he discovered to his horror, had been cloven in two, vertically, with a sword.

Hassell recalled one midshipman, climbing aboard from his boat and having his head severed from his neck and "fall[ing] on the deck before his body does."

But bodies fell rapidly on the other side as well; a Union report would claim that all but five of the crew on board were killed or captured. Captain Westervelt was shot in the leg; he tumbled overboard and would not be seen again until his body washed up on shore some days later.

The whole fight was over in five minutes, and the ship was in Wood's hands. Engineers quickly set themselves to the task of warming up the boilers. Other sailors split their duties between guarding prisoners, preparing to hold off additional defenders and trying to loose the boat from the wharf. But time was against the gallant crew. Already Fort Stevenson, on shore, was angling its cannons and riddling the craft with musket, grapeshot and solid shot. The side-wheeler's walking beam was soon disabled.

Commander Wood received further bad reports. The boiler's fires had completely cooled and would take at least an hour to build up steam. Heavy chains connecting the boat to a buoy would also require hours of work. Reluctantly, he gave the order to fire the ship.

The sailors abandoned the craft, taking their dead and some prisoners with them, and then lay on their oars while officers set fire to the lower decks. As they rowed away, they watched the *Underwriter* light the night until its powder rooms ignited, filling the air with the Fourth of July.

In the long term, there was little military significance to the raid. The city was left with two "inferior boats," but others would soon be added. Still, it showed that Dixie, though by this point outgunned and outmanned to a hopeless degree, still possessed the spunk and courage that makes its descendants so proud today.

Part IV

The Gilded Age and Beyond

A column detail of the Larry Moore House, East Front Street, New Bern. *Photo by the author.*

A NEW BERNIAN IN THE WHITE HOUSE

A former slave rose to a position of love and respect during the last half of the nineteenth century.

Did you know that New Bern had a man in the White House—and that he was black? Before the Civil War, he was owned by the Attmore family, so he very possibly lived in the Attmore-Oliver House. We know practically nothing about Arthur Simmons during this early period, nor even how he found himself working at the White House. Apparently he left New Bern for the nation's capital sometime after 1865.

Mary Norcott Bryan wrote of him in her circa 1912 book *A Grandmother's Recollections of Dixie* and remembered him fondly. "Quite a noted colored man was Arthur Simmons," she wrote. He was "a great friend of mine when I was a young lady, and many a waiter of dainties, interesting books, birds and squirrels did he bring me."

In an article for the 1904 November *Scribner's Magazine*, Thomas Nelson Page called him one of the last "[o]ld-time negroes" and gave this little portrait:

> *Whoever goes to the White House will find at the door of the executive offices an elderly and very stout negro door-keeper, with perfect manners, a step as soft as the fall of the leaf, and an aplomb which nothing can disturb. His name is Arthur Simmons, and, until toward the close of the war, he was a gentleman's servant in North Carolina; then he came North. He is, possibly, the oldest employee in the White House, having been appointed by General Grant during his first term, and having held his position, with the exception of a single term—that of General Harrison—to the present time. It is said that Mr. Cleveland's first appointment after his return to office was that of Arthur Simmons to his old post. Possibly, Mr. Cleveland had heard this story of him: Once, Arthur having learned that his old mistress had expressed a desire to see the President of the United States, invited her to Washington, met her at the station, saw to her comfort while in the city, arranged an interview with the President for her, and then escorted her back to take her train home.*

That woman was, of course, Miss Bryan. "You can imagine how my meeting him at Washington some years ago brought up many recollections of the past. My son was with me and Arthur could not do enough to make our visit interesting" she wrote. "In passing through several of the rooms we met

The Attmore-Oliver House. Before the Civil War, Arthur Simmons was a slave of the Attmore family. It is very likely here where he lived out his servitude as a house servant. The home is currently a museum owned by the New Bern Historical Society. *Photo by the author.*

a gentleman who proved to be the Secretary of War, [Russell] Alger. After our departure, he said to Arthur 'Who was that lady and gentleman who seemed glad to see you and to whom you were so very polite?' Arthur told him with much gusto, and Mr. Alger replied, 'We Northern people must have misunderstood the friendly relation that existed between master and slave.'"

Well, she had to make that happy-slave-and-master note in defense of her antebellum days, I suppose, but one must remember too, that there really were a number of incidents, both during and after the war, in which a strong and friendly bond was proven to exist between some slaves and their masters.

Arthur first began working for Ulysses S. Grant (who was president from 1869 to 1877) and remained in Washington at least through Theodore Roosevelt's administration—more than forty years.

Perusing newspapers during Roosevelt's presidency shows that he was much beloved. One article described a snowball fight started up in January 1904 by the president's son, Archie, who stumbled into the White House with an armful of said projectiles after school and started pelting him. "Simmons caught the fragments as they fell all over his ample person, and laughed the rest of the day at the fun," the article noted.

A Christmas article in the *Washington Times* (December 24, 1902) listed Arthur as "the faithful messenger, who has stood guard between the great public and the President for the past forty years." He was in line, the article said, for a present from Mrs. Roosevelt.

On one occasion, Teddy instructed him to pass the word that there would be no more smoking in the White House reception room. He got such an earful of profanity from angry, cigar-chomping congressmen that he appealed for help. The president complied, and a "No Smoking Allowed" sign was posted in the room. "When gentlemen come in with lighted cigars Arthur merely looks meaningly toward the sign," a paper noted.

THE BUGGYMOBILE

With a little more vision on the part of investors, Gilbert Waters's invention could have been more than a North Carolina curiosity.

If we had *just* listened to Gilbert Waters, we might all be driving Buggymobiles as proudly as we drink Pepsi (a New Bern invention) today. New Bern would be the real Detroit. Who knows, we might have even wound up with Motown. Or the Pistons. Think of *that.*

Gilbert S. Waters was the "Son" part of New Bern's G.H. Waters & Son Buggy and Carriage Factory in 1899. It was a fine career with no future, though no one knew so at the time. Not long before, Karl Benz in Germany had turned out his little horseless carriage, while in 1896, Henry Ford was selling his quadricycle, a queer contraption with a backfire that was heard 'round the world. Buggy makers everywhere looked nervously up when they heard it.

Not in New Bern. "Nonsense!" they growled, touching up their horse's behind. But Gilbert was different. In 1899, he'd gone to Baltimore and seen his first horseless carriage. Ideas and thoughts of fortune popped into Gilbert's head.

By 1900, he'd built his first "Buggymobile." For all intents and purposes, it was a horse buggy with a few modifications: he inserted a tiller to steer by; added a one-horsepower, gasoline-driven engine; and tossed the horse.

Above: The G.H. Waters & Son buggy factory, located on Broad Street, where the old firemen's station now stands. At center, in a white suit, is G.H. Waters. His son, Gilbert W., inventor of the Buggymobile, stands in a vest to his left. *Courtesy New Bern Firemen's Museum, New Bern, North Carolina.*

Right: Gilbert Waters and an unidentified passenger in the Buggymobile. *Courtesy North Carolina Office of Archives and History, Raleigh, North Carolina.*

It was compact—about seven feet long, three and a half feet wide and four feet tall. The gasoline engine was something of an innovation since many of the cars in that early day were steam driven.

Gilbert showed his invention off with a twelve-mile-per-hour jaunt down the main street, but potential backers were not impressed. "Too expensive!" they argued. "Too dangerous! Impractical!" One old dinosaur told him to keep his day job, for the horse and buggy would never go out of style; these gasoline-driven monstrosities would go the way of, well, dinosaurs.

It reminds one of the day a young Mark Twain offered to write a book for a New York publisher. The publisher frowned, waved at all the bookshelves in his office and shouted, "Books? What do I want with more books!" Of course, Mark Twain went on to write many books, and that publisher is known today for being a shortsighted fool.

Unfortunately—or fortunately, depending on whether you like living in New Bern or Detroit—Mr. Waters's story didn't end so well. With no money,

The Buggymobile as it is currently displayed at the North Carolina History Museum in Raleigh. *Photo by the author.*

his plans went flat. Meanwhile, up in Michigan, Henry Ford was landing fat cats who were convinced by his assembly line dreams.

Gilbert didn't give up his love of horseless transportation. He built a second Buggymobile in 1903, cannibalizing his original model. The new one topped a speed of thirty-five miles per hour and got forty miles on a gallon of gas. Thirty-six years later, it was still hopping about and doing fine. I have spoken on the phone with one of his great-nieces, who remembered getting rides in it. He even displayed it to the nation by firing it up on the national *We the People* radio show in New York City.

To the end of his life, Gilbert never got over his belief that, if he could only have found backing, he might have been another Henry Ford. And who knows? He may have been right.

His 1903 car is displayed at the state museum in Raleigh, a strange little buggy with a tiller in front and a motor under the seat. I have had the privilege of crawling around that car, taking pictures and measurements, and it is curious to see some of the old "spit and bailing wire" style of construction that took place in its creation. There are even a few pieces of wood apparently salvaged from other projects with old nails still in them. The Buggymobile looks to be in pretty good shape, and it wouldn't surprise me if it can still run. It doesn't take much to imagine Gilbert Waters chugging up and down past the Elks Building, like he did in the 1940s, feeling the wind in the remaining fronds of his hair and dreaming of what might have been.

The Athens Theatre

In honor of our self-proclaimed nickname, the "Athens of the South," we bring you the showcase Athens Theatre of New Bern.

"Conducted along the most progressive lines!" "No expense was spared!" "Others might be larger but none better!"

Such were the enthusiastic reviews in the *Illustrated City of New Bern, 1914*, and now Messieurs Lovick and Taylor were ready to bring you the greatest show on…um…Pollock Street.

The Athens Theatre opened its doors under the management of Hugh J. Lovick and Lee J. Taylor on April 12, 1911, "an event in the growth of the city," according to the *New Bern Weekly Journal*. Designed by the celebrated architect Herbert W. Simpson (he seems to have designed just about every building going up in those days) and paid for by William Blades, a lumber

In its original glory, the Athens Theatre included box seats and a grand curtain with a *Ben Hur* theme. *Courtesy North Carolina Office of Archives and History, Raleigh, North Carolina.*

baron who saw New Bern as his personal erector set (his buildings are everywhere), it was a $25,000 marvel.

Here are some of its original glories:

> *Entering the theatre the attractive interior is seen to have a scheme of color in green, the walls, furniture, seats and drapings being in that color. The theatre accommodates 700 people, of which the balcony provides room for 200…*
>
> *There are six dressing rooms, toilet and lavatory and property room… The drop curtain represents "Ben Hur Chariot Race" and with the scenery, was furnished by the Kansas City Scenic Co…*
>
> *At the sides of the stage are 4 boxes, 2 on each side…the chairs are of mahogany and leather.*

The foyer and façade were no small potatoes, either: "There are hundreds of electric lights and a large electric sign showing the name of the theatre

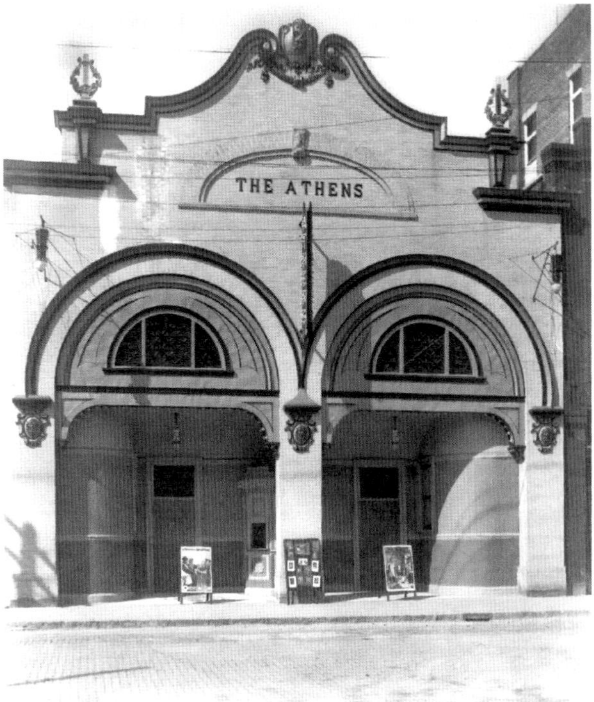

The Athens as it appeared in 1911. *Courtesy North Carolina Office of Archives and History, Raleigh, North Carolina.*

in red lights, and also two flaming arc lamps of 4,000 candle power each. The front entrance is in tiling and the mosaic settings in the floor represent 'Tragedy' and 'Comedy.'"

A *New Bern Weekly Journal* article from April 11, 1911, described the lighting machinery and a magnificent aluminum "silver screen." Strangely, it also spent a couple of paragraphs describing exits, fire hoses at the ready and an auxiliary lighting system of gas. Children at the dawn of the First World War must have been dazzled by the elaborate lights and surroundings as they laughed their way through vaudevilles and the antics of Charlie Chaplin and experienced the drama of John Barrymore.

If you weren't in the mood for a show during the summer, you might still pay a visit just to cool down. "The Athens is a perfect gem of a play house, cooled in summer by breezes from a score of electric fans. It is an ideal place to spend an hour or so of rest and recreation."

As talkies began to dominate the film industry, the Athens underwent major alterations to handle new equipment and to meet new laws. The ornate boxes were taken down and space in the balcony confiscated for the use of a metal projection booth.

Actress Sara Hand applies makeup before a 2009 production of *You Can't Take It With You*. *Photo by the author.*

Over the years, according to the theater's website, the Athens underwent changes in both management and names: the Show Shop, the Kehoe and the Tryon. The New Bern Civic Theatre purchased the building in February 1980 and renovated much of the interior. Its first show, Neil Simon's *The Star-Spangled Girl*, opened in September of the same year. To this day, thirty-five years later, NBCT holds regular performances of its own and has played host to other companies, including the North Carolinian Shakespeare Festival.

I should add that the NBCT is by no means the only company in town. Another community theater, the Rivertowne Repertory Players, operates from the stage at St. John's Masonic Lodge, while other smaller, private companies and schools put on musicals and plays at various stages and restaurant venues about town.

The Athens building façade looks tarnished today; its double-arched entrance is gone. Old rivets and bolts show where marquees and decorations used to be. But NBCT is working to raise funds to restore the building to its ancient glories. A diagonal stripe has been painted from top to bottom, making a kind of mural to show that the theater and its company still dream of a future in the past.

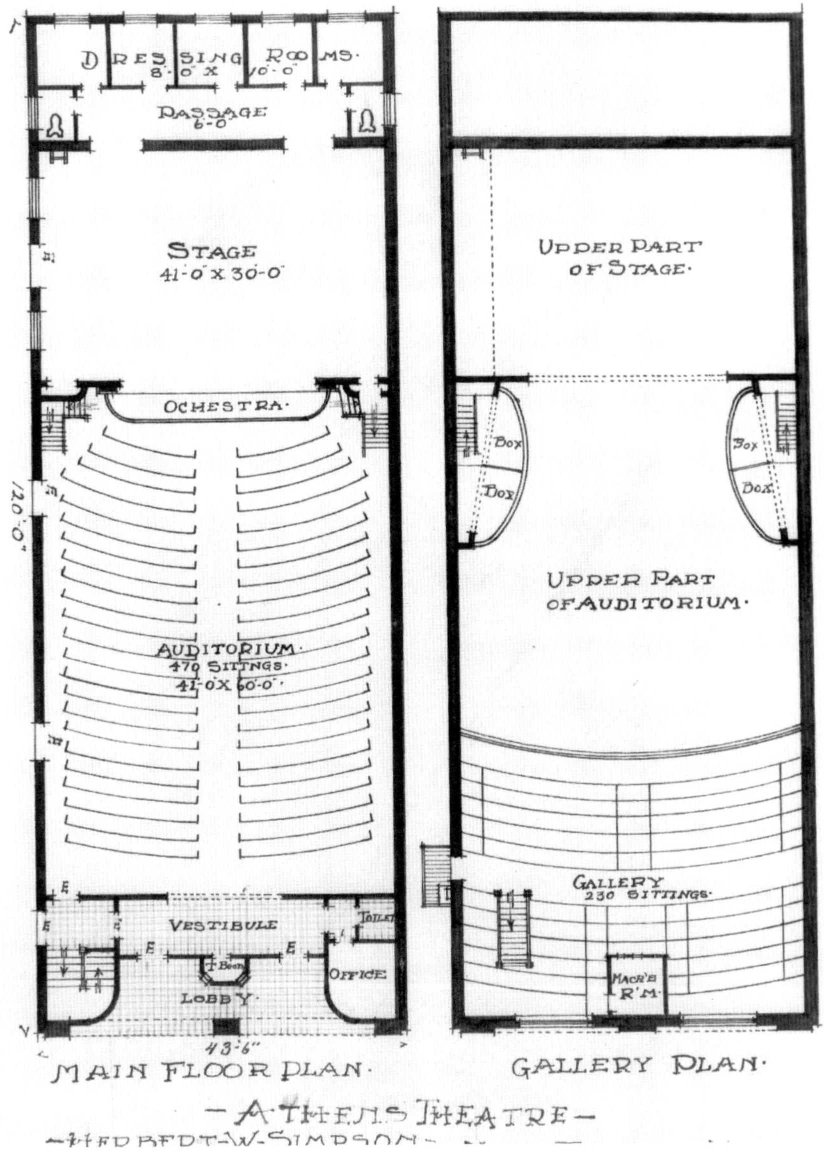

The original floor plan for the Athens. Its main differences today include the loss of the box seats and alterations in the lobby layout. *Courtesy North Carolina Office of Archives and History, Raleigh, North Carolina.*

The Deaths of Three Firemen

Two city firemen, we are told at the local fire museum, paid the ultimate price in the line of duty. A third—a county fireman—also gave his life in the cause of public safety. Here are their stories.

Johnnie Gaskill (July 11, 1875–November 6, 1904)

Johnnie Gaskill was a popular man. Born and raised in New Bern, the twenty-nine-year-old bachelor was one of the "best informed men on general topics in the city," according to the *New Bern Journal*. In other words, he could gab away on just about any subject you could name and actually keep you entertained. He must have been a hoot at the barbershop. His photograph suggests that he was a handsome and self-assured young man.

He was a fireman, a position envied in 1904. "To be a fireman in the old days was to be somebody," notes a welcome brochure at the New Bern Firemen's Museum. Uniforms and competitions, heroics and parading about on the horse-drawn fire engines, "[t]he Atlantic engine's sparkling nickel trim and the Button's highly polished brass" adding luster to it all—that is, the Atlantic Fire Company and the Button Fire Company. New Bern had two main fire companies then, and competition was hot between them. Often, when a fire alarm sounded, residents would turn out as much to see which company would beat the other to the fire as they would to see the blaze brought to bay.

Johnny Gaskill. *Courtesy New Bern Firemen's Museum, New Bern, North Carolina.*

Johnnie was a member of the Button Company—in fact, he was assistant fire chief. He was known for his fondness and handling of the fire horses, especially one named Jim. It is ironic, then, that tradition places him as the victim of a fire horse's kick.

Johnnie died of his "brief but very distressing illness" at twenty minutes before midnight, November 6, 1904, surrounded by his family (a mother, two sisters and two brothers) and friends. Probably his last hours were spent in a coma, as the *Journal* stated that "his end was peaceful."

The funeral was set for two days later, November 8, at the Centenary Methodist Church. The local minister presided, and members of both fire companies were required by their chiefs to attend. His coffin, buried under a sea of flowers, was lowered onto a wagon drawn by Jim himself, "an animal for which John had great affection and of which he often spoke in terms [of endearment]."

The troublesome part of this story is that it is very difficult to confirm whether his death was, indeed, fire-related or caused by a horse, using any locally available sources. Cemetery records state his cause of death as an "abscess of the liver." Certainly this could be caused by a strong horse kick. The North Carolina Fallen Firefighters Foundation (www.ncff.org) lists him as having been kicked in the head—a body part very far from the liver, so even here there is disagreement. The papers of the day describe his high reputation, his family and his lingering illness (it took two weeks to die, although the *Journal* stated that "from the first his case was desperate").

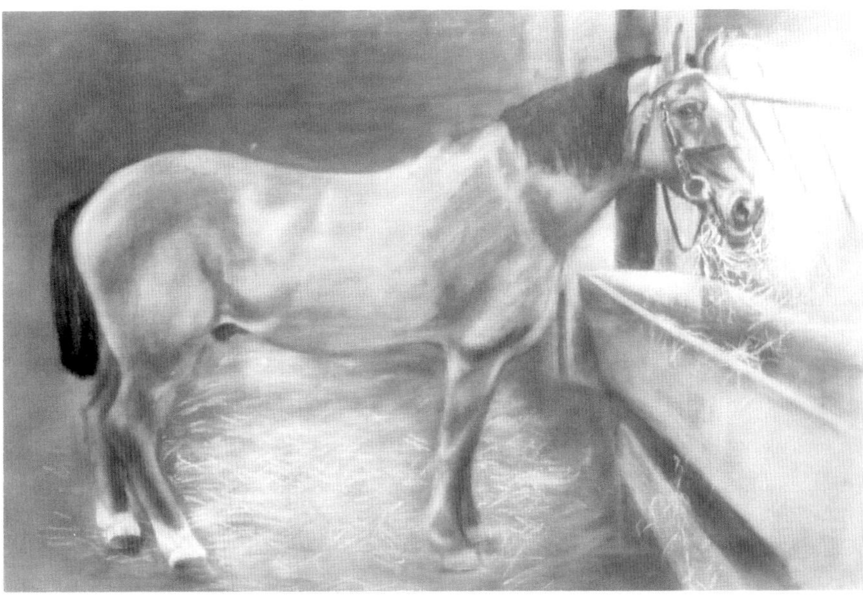

A portrait of Jim, Johnny Gaskill's favorite horse, hangs in the New Bern Firemen's Museum. "Old Jim" worked with the fire department for twenty-seven years, until 1909. *Courtesy New Bern Firemen's Museum, New Bern, North Carolina.*

Twenty-seven years later, the newspapers would report the firefighting death of Edgar B. Elliot as the first in the town's history—so perhaps Gaskill's death happened at a training exercise or at the station. The first mention we have of his death being caused by a fire horse is in the original literature of the New Bern Firemen's Museum back in the 1950s. No source here is listed, but there were men still alive who may have known Gaskill, and if the information was wrong, they certainly would have corrected it.

Is it possible that his fondness for the horses, his large send-off and the story of the favorite horse pulling his remains to their final destination somehow grew through the usual channels of oral legend into the generally accepted story of today?

Be that as it may, the town thought that he was more than worthy of a hero's farewell.

Edgar B. Elliott (May 22, 1904–June 10, 1931)

The day that Johnnie Gaskill died, Edgar B. Elliott was not quite eight months old. It would be nicely dramatic to imagine him coming from a firefighting family and that he and his mother had attended Johnnie's funeral, so many years before. It would be romantic to think of his mother suppressing a mysterious chill as the casket was closed and of her telling tales of Johnnie Gaskill's heroics to her young son as he grew up. However, he grew up in Jones County, and his father was a cotton buyer. So we'll have to let that fantasy fade away.

In 1931, Edgar was twenty-seven years old. He had been a fireman for seven years. Only two years before that, on December 1, 1922, New Bern experienced the worst fire in its (or the state's) history when nearly one-fourth of the town burned down in a few hours. Edgar had been eighteen then and was possibly a witness to the event. Perhaps it had inspired him to join.

Like Johnnie, Edgar was a bachelor. In June 1931 he was just a month shy of twenty-seven. He was also a Button Company man and an officer (assistant captain of the hose). He seemed to have gotten along well with his fellow firefighters, but I've seen no evidence that he had quite the charisma or popularity of Johnnie Gaskill. If the museum's photograph of him is indicative of character, he seems to have been a fairly serious, studious young man. His comrades would remember him as "a man of intrepid spirit, never hesitating to do his duty as he saw it and always in the hottest part of the fire," according to the *New Bernian* on June 12, 1931. His friends had given him the sobriquet "Chubby," and he was employed as a salesman

Edgar B. Elliot. *Courtesy New Bern Firemen's Museum, New Bern, North Carolina.*

at the town's popular New Bern Candy Company. Picture or not, just how serious could a guy named "Chubby" be, working at a candy store?

Chubby lived in an apartment with his mother, Lucy Harper Elliott, at 24 George Street in one of the oldest houses in town—a brick, two-story structure that had originally been the elaborate stable of the colonial governor, William Tryon. It had been completed along with his Palace in 1770 and had survived long after the governor's mansion had burned down in 1798. The Palace, in 1931, existed only as a foundation buried under the ground: George Street ran right through the middle of it and onto a bridge. Today, 24 George Street is part of the Tryon Palace Historic Sites and Gardens, restored to its original stable motif and nestled humbly to the west of the splendidly rebuilt Palace.

Chubby may not have been sleeping well the early hours of June 10, 1931—the weather that day had peaked at a more-than-balmy eighty-eight degrees; probably the windows were open in an attempt to at least put movement to the hot night air.

Before New Bern's revitalization days, the Trent River was lined with docks, warehouses and fish markets rather than the hotels and manicured parks of today. At the east end of Craven Street, the New Bern Building Supply had a store and large metal warehouse; behind that was the E.K. Bishop and Company wholesaler. Among its holdings was a large fertilizer storage warehouse, set on pilings over the water. Lining the docks around and behind them were barges, yachts and other boats, tied up.

On Middle Street, one block to the north, a number of small markets were built over the wharves. One of those was Lupton Fish & Oyster Company, at 12 Middle Street. Its owner was a lively local character named Mack Lupton (in the future he would become a leading advocate for the city's development and one of its most popular mayors). Apparently a kind of "burn the candle at both ends" man, Lupton was working at the market that morning when, shortly after three o'clock, he noticed smoke coming from the warehouses to the east. He quickly called in the alarm. But even before firemen could arrive, bringing every piece of equipment in the city, the fire was already belching through the roof.

An unusual bit of luck was with the town: though the wind was strong, it was blowing in a southerly direction, pushing the fire toward the river. Had the wind come from a different direction, the whole business district would have been endangered. But what was luck for the town was not so for the boats on the riverside. Mack Lupton made his way to the riverfront and started shouting for anyone in them to get out of harm's way.

The *Connecticut*, a one-thousand-ton barge owned by the Southern Transportation Company of Norfolk, was one of the craft moored that

Fireman "Chubby" Elliot resided in this apartment building (photo taken about 1930) with his mother before his death. Today the building has been restored to its original condition as the Tryon Palace stables. *Courtesy New Bern Firemen's Museum, New Bern, North Carolina.*

early morning at the warehouse. R.N. Quidley, a Cape Hatteras resident (Quidleys reside there to this day), was captain of the ship and lived on board along with his first mate, Cecil Henley. Also living on board was the captain's wife, their young daughter, Mercede, and a Spitz dog. They were awakened by Lupton's shouts. Grabbing his wife and child, Quidley dashed for the dock with Henley, only to find that the portion of the barge between them and safety was already engulfed in flames, set afire by airborne debris.

Another barge, the *Diamond State*, was also manned, by African American watchman Tobe Roberts. Seeing the warehouse ablaze, he chose to dive into the water, away from the conflagration. Although he injured his ankle in the act, he was able to swim some fifty yards to the neighboring J.R. Meadows lot, where he was pulled from the water to safety.

At 24 George Street, the 3:30 a.m. fire alarm had jolted Chubby awake. As he sat up in bed, he tried to determine from which part of the city the alarm had sounded. He may already have picked up the pungent odor of burning wood wafting through his window.

Dressing quickly, he stumbled down the steps and into the street. Marion Stewart, a fellow fireman, was waiting in his car with another friend, Ural Rhodes. Chubby climbed inside and they sped off.

The sky to the east was already lit up with dancing orange light, blotted out here and there with clouds of roiling smoke. As they pulled up to the scene, they could see hundreds of people already gathering to watch the show, while firemen from both the Button and Atlantic Companies rolled out hoses and decided how to tackle the fire. Fire Chief William J. Smith was calling out orders, and Ural and Marion hurried his way. But Chubby's ears perked up at a sound from behind the inferno—someone, he realized, was calling for help.

It is not entirely clear what happened after that. But apparently Chubby hurried out to the docks, where he saw the Quidley family, trapped on the *Connecticut*. There was no way to reach them from the wharf so, although he could not swim and was encumbered with his heavy firefighting uniform, he untied a skiff from the dock and started rowing toward the barge through a rain of burning embers.

Mack Lupton, still on shore, happened to look out about that time and see a fireman standing on a small boat, with "both hands uplifted in an appeal for help." The boat, he recalled later, was floating at an angle, with the stern against the now burning dock and the bow bumped against the burning end of the barge. The boat itself was burning on both ends. "The only chance that guy has is to jump overboard," he thought. By now, other firemen were coming around the docks, untying boats and setting them adrift in hopes they would float out of harm's way. Firemen Guy Lupton and Mark Malone called for him to join in this activity. While he helped, he described what he had seen. But the firemen were too busy to pay close attention. "That was probably George Harper," one told him. "He was on a skiff cutting the *Etta Kahn* loose, you know." At the moment, Lupton gave it little more thought. They were probably right. It had been Harper, on board a skiff, who had called him to aid.

Later, the two Luptons and Malone would ride a skiff to where Mack had seen the fireman—all they would find was the charred bottom of a boat, afloat on the water.

Meanwhile, the firemen continued to battle the blaze. Two men were injured fighting flames on the roof, and numerous others received minor burns. Of particular concern was a freight car stacked with powdered lye—not necessarily dangerous if the flames reached it, but if hit with the copious water being poured out it could have given off deadly fumes.

In the end, the fire was brought under control, with losses contained to the warehouse and several boats (including some that, after being cut loose, had drifted back into the burning docks). Damages were set at $200,000, and it was declared the worst fire in recent memory.

Considering their job done, the firemen packed up and went home. No one saw Chubby. They assumed that he had gone home, as well.

The New Bern Candy Company opened for business as usual, but Chubby didn't show. At home, his mother Lucy must have guessed that he was with firefighting friends until time to work. But when he didn't come home for lunch, she grew worried and notified the Button Company.

It was quickly ascertained that he hadn't been seen since he first arrived at the fire. Someone remembered Mack Lupton's story of a fireman on a burning skiff. Poles and chains were used to drag and probe the river along the docks, while others poked about the warehouse ruins. Dynamite, a favorite tool of the firemen of that age, was brought in and the end of the dock blown up in the hopes that it would turn up Elliott's body.

Chubby Elliott remained elusive. The Thursday edition of the *New Bernian* reported that a fruitless search had been going on since early the day before. He was finally found in the late afternoon, after twenty-five hours of searching, near the slip where the *Diamond State* barge had burned. Fireman Luther Taylor discovered him while prodding the bottom of the two-fathom-deep water with a pike pole from a rowboat. It had been thirty-six hours since the first alarm.

His funeral was conducted at First Baptist, his church, on the afternoon of June 12. In tribute to him, most of the merchants in town closed their businesses during the hour of the service.

A June 13 article gives an interesting glance at how the fireman-hero's interment was conducted:

> *After the service at the church, the body was taken to Cedar Grove cemetery on the draped Button truck, on which he had frequently ridden to fires. The truck and the fire house will be draped in mourning for 30 days.*
>
> *Numerous floral wreaths, including many handsome designs, were taken to the cemetery in the Atlantic fire truck and in the Morehead City fire truck. Over the casket was a beautiful blanket of lilies and fern, sent by fellow members of the Button company. Large designs were sent by the Atlantic company, the New Bern Firemen's Relief board, M.T. Mahone, of Charlotte, of the Eureka Fire Hose company and the American Lay-France Foamite company, who was here during the search for Elliott's body.*
>
> *Members of the Junior Order of American Mechanics, to which the deceased also belonged, conducted the burial ritual at the graveside, led by Councillor G. A. Barden. Dr. Haywood offered the benediction. A firing squad from Battery D, of which the deceased was a former member, fired a salute over the grave. Taps were sounded by a batteryman.*
>
> *The fire whistle then sounded three taps, in closing tribute to the departed fireman. From 2:45 to 3 p.m., just previous to the funeral, the fire bell had been tolled, and for 20 minutes it tolled as the procession moved from the church to the cemetery.*

He was buried at Cedar Grove Extension Cemetery.

Gerald O'Neal Tilghman (February 4, 1921-November 6, 1973)

He was with the county West of New Bern Fire Company, rather than a city organization, and so you will not find his plaque at the New Bern Firemen's Museum. Still, he was a local man who gave his life in the line of duty, and his story should be told.

Gerald O'Neal Tilghman had been with the company about six years. In 1973, he was the traffic officer and was fifty-two years old. Current (2011) assistant chief Cleve Woolard remembered him as "a super-nice guy, always willing to help anybody," and who was "very dedicated to the fire service." He was known as a family-oriented man, enjoying life with his wife and two children, Betty Sue and Ronnie. A volunteer, he earned his living in civil service at Cherry Point.

On the evening of November 6, 1973—ironically, the sixty-ninth anniversary of Johnnie Gaskill's death—the fire department received a call regarding a vehicle fire at Al's Auto Salvage on Oaks Road. The fire trucks pulled out of their base at 900 Chelsea Road and headed down Highway 17 toward the fire.

It was Gerald's job to help clear traffic for the fire trucks, and upon arriving at the intersection of Highway 17 and Simmons Street, he climbed out of the car and, in the growing dark, began to stop traffic to give the trucks clearance. Cars pulled over as the fire truck approached, "lights flashing and sirens screaming," according to a *Sun-Journal* article. But one car—a yellow Ford coupe—did not slow down at all. Driven by Walter T. Bell, a Camp LeJeune marine, it sped straight toward him, oblivious to his presence. Gerald saw it come and tried to dodge, but it was too late. The resulting collision sent him flying sixty-seven feet and killed him instantly.

Bell pulled over, but not until he had gone another 475 feet down the road. Police reported that he had left no skid marks either before or after he struck Gerald, so he apparently had not even attempted to stop. Perhaps he hadn't seen the fireman at all.

Police gave him a blood-alcohol test, and he passed it, recording a 0.08 level (the drunken driving law of the time required a 1.00 level). Still, he was charged with public drunkenness, driving under the influence and failure to yield the right of way to an emergency vehicle. Later, the charge of manslaughter was added.

The fire alarm turned out to be false.

Tilghman is buried at Greenleaf Cemetery. His son Ronnie joined the fire company when he turned eighteen and served with West of New Bern for several years.

The West of New Bern company soon moved into a new building constructed at its original site. It was named in Tilghman's honor in 1975, and a memorial plaque stands at the station.

WHEN GERMAN SOLDIERS CAME TO NEW BERN

Glenburnie Park was the site of a German encampment during much of World War II.

There may not have been battles in America during World War II, but there *were* firefights not far from land. German U-boats were having regular turkey shoots up and down the Atlantic coast, and more than one American ship nailed itself a U-boat, as well.

I have toured a World War II–era submarine and am sure that I would have gone bats in one of those things, trapped underwater and knowing what my chances of escape were if someone punched holes in my craft while we were under the sea. If the movie *Das Boot* was typical, those sailors must have lived a life of terror.

Again, though there may not have been real battles in America during World War II, there were plenty of German soldiers here. By 1945, in fact, there were 387,000 Axis power soldiers in America—10,000 of them tramping about, often without guards, in North Carolina. And as many as 308 were moving around New Bern. They weren't running around with guns, at least, but a few of them carried axes.

Why haven't you heard more about them? Well, they were prisoners of war. The government was careful not to make a big deal about it, because it didn't want to start a panic; there were residents of New Bern during the war who didn't even know they were here.

The first German prisoners to come through New Bern were U-boat men, probably from the *U-352*, which was sunk off the coast of North Carolina on May 9, 1942. No papers record the event. It was kept quiet at the time (partly to keep Germany from learning exactly what had

Some of the barracks at Camp Battle. *Courtesy Robert McCall.*

happened), but the late "Shoot" Hall of New Bern, who was driving a bus in those days, related the event to friends in town during his last years. His tale was that a bus arrived with naked men—German prisoners. He was kind enough, he said, to go into the Kress Department Store and get them all pajamas to wear.

Those men didn't stay in New Bern; they were shipped to Fort Bragg and, after the summer, were moved on to Charleston. As for the *U-352* itself, it is a popular site for divers of intermediate skill, and a scale model of it is on display as part of the Pine Knoll Shores Aquarium near Atlantic Beach.

Clearly, with numbers in the hundreds of thousands, most Axis prisoners were not captured from submarines off the coast. They came from Europe and Africa. As the war ground on, more and more Germans were being captured in the field—in a few cases, whole armies. The American allies were running out of places to keep them. The United States, meanwhile, was in the process of shipping thousands of soldiers overseas in transport ships. Since those ships would otherwise come back empty, they took to loading them with prisoners of war. Once in America, these men were scattered across most of the nation in main camps and branch camps.

America was undergoing a serious labor shortage at the time: large numbers of the workforce were tramping about Europe and the Pacific with guns. The government decided that it only made sense to take advantage of this massive manpower that otherwise would be sitting in frustrating uselessness behind barbed wire and put them to work. And so the prisoners were farmed out to factories, farms, military bases and forestry services to keep them from idleness and the nation from idling.

North Carolina had two main camps: Camp Butner, north of Durham, and Fort Bragg. Sixteen branch camps were set up across the state at the time. New Bern's branch camp was named Camp Battle in honor of a Civil War general and former New Bern mayor and was located on the grounds that today are Glenburnie Park and the city waterworks. You can still find the original camp foundations under some of the pavilions there. It was wooded and surrounded with barbed wire; inside were a number of CCC-type barracks with mess halls, a canteen, a recreation hall and a dispensary.

It started as a camp for American soldiers. The 111th Regiment had opened the camp in February 1942. The 111th is one of the oldest regiments in the nation, started by Benjamin Franklin in 1745. Robert McCall, a veteran of the regiment now living in Atlantic, recalled that the camp was "just bare. Trees—pine trees," when the men first arrived. They lived in tents until wood-framed barracks were built, covered over in tar paper.

Their duties consisted of drilling and performing guard duties about New Bern and the surrounding areas as far away as the Atlantic coast. In November 1943, the regiment moved on, called to the Pacific Theater of the war.

The camp sat fallow for about nine months until August 3, 1944, when the first POWs arrived. They were remarkably well treated under the guidelines of the Geneva Convention: during most of the war, they received 3,700 calories a day—the same as American soldiers. American prisoners in Axis-held camps did not fare nearly so well.

The prisoners had religious privileges, with evangelical services run by a POW in camp and Catholic services performed by a priest in town, probably Monsignor Irwin from St. Paul's. As a whole, they were apparently not very devout: only about thirty attended Irwin's services, and only fifteen showed up for Protestant services. Martin Luther must have been rolling in his grave.

Camp Battle POWs were put to work on local farms, factories and in the nearby forests; a few worked at the town fertilizer factory; and at one point, thirty-two were working the grounds at the National Cemetery. When private citizens used them, it was their responsibility to pick up their workers at the gate and then bring them back at night. A number of New Bernians remember, as children, seeing these prisoners work.

Gene McIlwean is a semiretired farmer living near the Weyerhauser plant who recalled those German workers. His family runs the McIlwean Turf Farm, but in those days tobacco was the primary crop. "I had come home from school," he recalled. "There were several sitting in the front of the yard on the lawn, waiting for my uncle to come out and pick them up and take them back to the camp. They didn't speak any English. As a six-year-old kid, I thought they sounded like some kind of quick talking and jabbering, and I couldn't understand it at all!" He remembers that one of the workers was a midget, "just a head taller than me."

A favorite of the McIlwean family was a clockmaker named Gus. This prisoner had a fairly good handle on English and took a strong liking to the children—especially Bunny McIlwean, a little girl who reminded him of his own daughter back home. Sometimes Gus brought gifts—he made rings for each of the children out of spoons (Gene lost his to a classmate the next day when he took it to school) and occasionally took nonfunctioning clocks back to camp. Returning a day or so later, he had worked magic on them and got them working.

Max Armstrong is another New Bernian who watched the Germans assist his father. Although his father ran a nursery, he also poured concrete for people in town. "We had these German prisoners to fill up the cement mixer

The 111th Regiment occupied Camp Battle before it was used as a prisoner of war camp. Here, members of the 111th pose in front of their barracks with a Browning machine gun. *Courtesy Robert McCall.*

with the proper ingredients for whatever kind of work we were doing," Armstrong recalls, "and these people were really smart. When you showed them something, they picked up on it; usually just in one time."

Max remembers how one of the prisoners would go on break each day, walking to a local store. Often, Max would go with him. "That German prisoner of war would buy the most kinds of candy that he could get for a penny or a nickel…I remember the squirrel nuts, and Mary Janes, and stuff like that; you'd get a pretty big handful for a nickel. Well…he would come back and distribute the candy he bought, kind of equally, among the other two. They always shared."

Gene remembers one frightening event—for a six-year-old, at least—though he suspects that he may have been the victim of a joke:

> *This one particular afternoon, we came home from school. My brother and I jumped out of the car. We were gonna go see the Germans! And so we took off down across the farm. It was probably, like, three or four football fields—about three football fields down to the back of the farm, which was quite a ways. And my dad had them working along the edge of the highland and the river floodplain area, where they were cutting wood—this was in the wintertime—they were cutting wood that was going to be used next summer for curing tobacco.*

> *These German soldiers were spread out along a ridgeline, probably 150 yards. When we came upon the site, we came up to one end, where there was a couple of soldiers working there. Gus is standing there, so I'm going over to where Gus is chopping wood with a long axe, and they're cutting down trees and cutting the limbs off. We didn't have chainsaws back in those days, by the way!*
>
> *So I was standing there, watching, and this one soldier that was right near, between where I was standing and Gus was standing. It looked like what I would call about an eighteen-year-old kid now, about five-foot-three, not real stocky. So he's chopping wood and I'm standing there watching, you know. Just for no reason at all, he pulled his axe up into the air, and he made a statement that scared me so much I couldn't move. He said, "Me kill!" That's what it sounded like to me. And I was so scared I couldn't move. And he was holding the axe up in the air. I thought he meant he was going to kill me!* [laughs] *Or he was trying to scare me. I knew it was more like he was probably trying to scare me. He may have said something in German that* sounded *like that. But anyway, it scared me.*
>
> *Gus went over and grabbed him by the arm and said, "Hey!" And said something to him in German and made him put the axe back down. And then he took me and he led me up the ridgeline a little bit. Said, "Look, you go over there where your father is."*

Over all, German POWs in America were well behaved and attempted very few escapes. Where could they go? They were an ocean and thousands of miles from friendly territory. New Bern had a minor event when three German workers sabotaged a fertilizer machine by throwing a broken shovel and a brick into it. Not quite up to par with *Hogan's Heroes*.

New Bern also had one escapee who managed to remain unfound for a year. His name was Paul Schmidt, a former auto mechanic from Ernsfthal. He had been captured at Caen, France.

Schmidt was considered to be unstable. On April 12, 1945—the same day President Franklin Delano Roosevelt died—he fled from a work detail on the Old Pollocksville Road near James City. A hunt was made, and the Federal Bureau of Investigation called in, but it wasn't until November 27, 1946, that he was finally found—in a swamp, hanged by his belt from a tree. The cause of death was "assumed to have been the result of the prisoner's demented state," according to a report. He is buried along with a handful of other World War II prisoners at Fort Bragg.

Known Nazis, who tended to be more zealous than their fellow prisoners, were kept separate from them (there was, in fact, a special place at Camp

Butner for them). The prisoners seemed fairly content with their plight; still, they looked forward to going home. But when the war ended on May 7, 1945, the prisoners stayed. The country still needed their labor, and some camps were set up with special training classes in an attempt to convince them to embrace American-style democracy before they went home.

Camp Battle did not officially close until November 1946.

ST. LUKE'S AND GOOD SHEPHERD HOSPITALS CLOSE THEIR DOORS

These two hospitals served the New Bern community—one, the whites and the other, the African Americans—through the end of the segregation years.

St. Luke's still stands on Broad Street, its Romanesque "ST LVKE'S" chiseled into its façade, though much of the building is empty and waiting for a purchaser and renovation. Nearby, Good Shepherd still stands as well, less classic in its design and operating as an assisted living home. Until 1963, both were hospitals, and many a New Bernian can trace his or her birth to one of these two buildings. Following are a few of their stories.

St. Luke's Hospital as it appeared in 1916. *Courtesy New Bern Historical Society.*

St. Luke's was the accomplished dream of two area physicians, Drs. J.F. Patterson and R. DuVal Jones, who had it built in 1915. The architect Burrett Stevens designed it as a modern hospital but in a classical style of brick and limestone to blend into the town's historic aura. It opened its doors in 1916.

A couple of smaller hospitals hung their shingles up in town on occasion, but for many years it was always understood that St. Luke's was *the* hospital of the place.

It is odd to imagine, but by 1942 there were only thirty-five beds available in St. Luke's. The federal government stepped in at that time, shouldering the responsibility of enlarging the building and increasing the beds to eighty-six—more than double its old occupancy. Soon in financial straits, the hospital got the attention of a Newark, New Jersey convent.

The Sisters of St. Joseph of Mercy purchased the hospital and took it over in August 1944. Twelve sisters moved to New Bern and operated the hospital under the guidance of Bishop Eugene McGinnis and Sister Catherine Flannery, their first administrator. Crosses were hung in every room, and the sisters hired additional nurses, many of them from among the wives of soldiers.

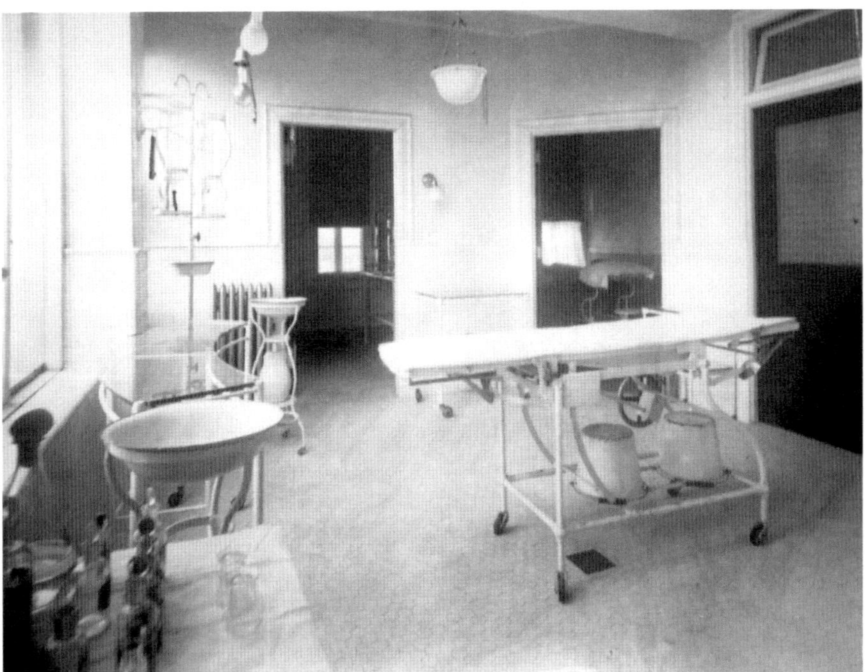

The operating room in St. Luke's Hospital as it appeared in 1916. *Courtesy New Bern Historical Society.*

Good Shepherd Hospital was one of the positive things that arose from the New Bern Fire of 1922. That fire, starting at a lumber mill and a private residence at both ends of town in the morning hours of December 1, destroyed almost one-fourth of the town. Nearly all the damage was in the black community. As a precaution, St. Luke's, not far from the blaze, was evacuated. Emergency hospitals were quickly set up.

St. Cyprian's Episcopal Church, the African American sister of Christ Church downtown, was commandeered. Reverend R.I. Johnson worked diligently alongside New Bern doctor Joseph Latham, who would put in thirty-six hours' straight work. Before the day was out, the fire would sweep almost past the church's front door. St. Peter's AME Zion Church, within sight, just a couple of blocks away, would burn down, though St. Cyprian's would survive unscathed.

The entire fire resulted in only one casualty: Harriet Reeves, an elderly African American woman. However, the disaster got Reverend Johnson thinking about the inadequacy of care for his fellow African Americans in New Bern. Julius Parham, a former New Bern alderman, once said, "The Rev. R.I. Johnson of St. Cyprian realized the need for a hospital for black people. Through his efforts the Episcopal dioceses built Good Shepherd

Good Shepherd Home, formerly a hospital for the black community. *Photo by the author.*

Hospital which served the people until better medical care became available to them."

Initial ideas strike like lightning, but they sometimes gain momentum like glaciers. Good Shepherd would be one of those slow-moving behemoths, an idea that would percolate in fits and starts of fundraising and planning for sixteen years. Reverend Johnson himself was the main moving force, raising funds primarily through the Episcopal Dioceses of Pennsylvania ($25,000), the Duke Endowment ($15,000) and the Diocese of East Carolina ($10,000). Finally, in 1938, it opened its doors at 603 West Street. Seven patients were admitted the first day.

Ozzie Trevor Faison, administrator of the hospital in its later years, recalled the original staff:

> *The staff consisted of both black and white. Dr. H.B. Wadsworth, Dr. R.N. Duffy, Dr. O.A. Kafer and Dr. C.H. Ashford. The black doctors were Dr. Hunter Fisher, Dr. William Martin and Dr. William Mann. We had three black doctors here at that time. They were the ones serving on the original staff at Good Shepherd Hospital. All other doctors in the community and surrounding area had courtesy privileges to serve. This hospital continued to operate for some time. Soon the staff became more involved and other people joined the staff. That was the first stage of the Good Shepherd Hospital.*
>
> *Rev. Johnson was the hospital's first head of administration, a job he continued until his death in August, 1946. Faison was hired to run the 52-bed facility a month later.*

Though Faison had no administrative experience regarding medical care, he quickly learned the ropes and kept the hospital afloat through difficult times. He was able to gain accreditation for the hospital in 1960—no small feat. Dr. Lula Disosway, whom he would hire in 1955 as medical director, once called him a miracle worker who had "an uncanny genius for stretching dollars," according to an Associated Press article from 1964. The article noted:

> *Accreditation is hard to get and hard to keep. In professional circles, it is evidence enough that a hospital has earned public confidence. In professional circles it is, too, a matter of approving wonder that Good Shepherd has maintained accreditation standards and at the same time functioned within a modest budget, battled successfully to keep its charges to patients well below current levels, while rendering more than the average proportion of charity service.*

> *Good Shepherd has no endowment to smooth its financial path; no wealthy benefactor to assume any part of its burden. It must live on revenues from patients, supplements by modest contributions from its sponsor and other religious groups, both Negro and white, plus nominal donations, grants and fees from foundations and agencies, such as welfare, which call upon its services. These add up to a budget within which few 53-bed hospitals could operate.*

Disosway herself was a miraculous catch. A New Bern native, she had spent several years as a medical missionary to China and Alaska for the Episcopal Church. By 1964, she was one of the few whites employed at the hospital.

Disosway was especially devoted to the birthing of babies and their early care; this had been her passion in China and would continue to be so even after Good Shepherd was closed, working closely with poor families in the black community.

At its peak of operation, Good Shepherd had thirteen nurses, seven aides and three orderlies, working under nursing head Laura Moore. The patients' rooms, according to that same AP article, were "larger than [in] most present-day hospitals" and were "nicely furnished and attractively painted."

By the early 1960s, large changes were coming. St. Luke's was struggling financially to survive. Sister Helena, administrator of the hospital at the time, announced on April 1, 1962, that she would have to close the doors in two weeks. The community responded by raising funds to purchase the hospital. Craven County Hospital took over on May 15, 1962. The *New Bern Sun-Journal* eulogized:

> *In each room of St. Luke's Hospital is the outline of a cross where paint had not faded under the Crucifix that had hung on that spot.*
>
> *These crosses on a wall in each room remain as a reminder to all who enter the hospital of the service that was rendered those who had stayed in that room before recovering from illness or injury under the care of the Sisters of St. Joseph.*

The sisters, some of whom had served at St. Luke's for eighteen years, were relocated to other St. Joseph's charities around the nation.

During its last years, it had treated an average of ninety people a day and, during its history, had brought 7,289 babies into the world. The obituaries of the 1950s and early 1960s are filled with the names of souls who spent their last breath gazing upon those outline-forming crosses.

Carolina East, in its original incarnation as Craven County Hospital, replaced previous hospitals in the New Bern community. *Photo by the author.*

Less than a year later, the county hospital was moved across town to a much bigger and newer facility. It held its elaborate grand opening on April 22, 1963. The new $2 million, one-hundred-bed building was dedicated by Governor Terry Sanford, who cut the ribbon and gave one of those governorlike speeches to the crowd. According to the *Sun-Journal* that day, he "expressed the wish that the new Craven County Hospital might find its most service in bringing about the recovery of those ill rather than a prime demand in serving those who meet death and destruction on the highways." It sounds almost biblical and makes you wonder what med he'd forgotten to take that morning.

More than 6,500 people came to witness the dedication and explore the bowels of the historic new edifice (built, strangely enough, at the site of a former prison). School students were given time off to attend, except for members of the marching band, who had to show up to play. Perhaps they performed a patient's suite?

County attorney Lawrence A. Stith presented the new hospital to its first chairman of the board, Luther J. Eubank. Governor Sanford concluded the program by cutting the ribbon, and the visitors flowed in to visit the antiseptically new halls, touring the building independently or through organized tours until 8:00 p.m. No patients were disturbed, by the way, as they wouldn't arrive until the twenty-fifth.

That price, $2 million, translates into about $13.9 million today. It resulted in one of the most modern noneducational hospitals in the state. Still, the governor said, it was a bargain: per bed, the whole place cost about $1,600, which was quite a bit cheaper than the national average of $22,000 per bed.

In this new age of growing integration, the hospital was open to both whites and blacks. No longer serving as great a need, Good Shepherd would bow to the county hospital and close its doors in 1967.

Since 1963, the county hospital has changed its name to Craven Regional Medical Center and then again to Carolina East. New construction has virtually swallowed up the original building and has added sections enough to bring it to 350 beds, nearly all of them in private rooms.

Finally, What If?

A little tweak in history here or there, and New Bern could have wound up a very different place.

Maybe it's all in how the cards play out.

During the Civil War, New Bern was—comparatively speaking—a pretty big town. Statewide, it was smaller only than Wilmington and more than twice

The city hall clock tower and the Christ Church steeple rise above a morning fog lifting off the Neuse River, as seen from the opposite shore. *Photo by the author.*

the size of Charlotte. Even Atlanta—which war, time and Margaret Mitchell would enshrine in romance and tragedy—had only 9,554 residents—only a little more than twice our size of 5,432.

But look at us now. We (29,524) are just over 7 percent the size of Atlanta's population (420,003) and only about 4 percent of Charlotte's (765,555). How did they get so big, and why did we stay so small?

There are probably hundreds of little reasons. But history *can* hinge on singular events. Take Lincoln's assassination. Take Waterloo. Sometimes I wonder what New Bern might be today if certain events had gone another way. Here are three candidates:

- 1788: New Bern remains the capital of North Carolina. Ruffians across the state are pressing hard to move the capital inland, toward a location more central to the population. However, moneyed influences along the coast and infighting among the inland population work together to defeat any such bill.
- 1905: Two years after the appearance of the second Buggymobile, local entrepreneur and carriage maker Gilbert Waters convinces North Carolina industrialists to raise the money he needs to build a factory in New Bern. By 1907, Waters's cars, inspired by the Buggymobile prototype, are rolling off the assembly line.
- 1923: Caleb Bradham is able to shore up his popular soft drink empire with business loans and investments. Though teetering on the brink of bankruptcy over sugar prices, Pepsi-Cola survives in New Bern, while smart marketing ensures that the city will forever be its corporate home.

There are other events that, I think, might have altered our history in significant, though less dramatic ways. What if enough extra troops had poured into town early in March 1862, providing the men needed to properly man the lines at Fort Thompson? If the South had won the Battle of New Bern, and the city's defenses had continued to be improved, what effect (if any) would it have had on the war? Would the breadbasket of North Carolina have been better able to feed the South's hungry troops? Could the town have held up as long as Wilmington? Would this extra port of entry have had any real effect on supplies to the materially poor South? This might have had little effect on New Bern today, but it might have had a huge effect on the nation.

What about the Fire of 1922, which burned down almost the entire black section of the city? As a result, many African Americans migrated to other states (many to Ohio). A resulting change was that New Bern's demographics changed from a city whose population was mostly black to one that was mostly white. Wind, a lack of equipment and firemen (most of whom were in Raleigh watching a championship high school football game) and a "red herring" fire at a lumberyard on the riverbank all conspired to allow a little chimney fire to take out one-fourth of the town. What if that chimney had not caught fire at all? Or what if the firemen had been quick enough to keep it from spreading?

There are probably another dozen "what ifs," each one having the possibility of having altered the town in small (but significant) or big ways. What if we *were* still the home base of Pepsi…or a "Little Detroit"? What if, today, Tryon Palace—not the rebuilt one but the original building (for, as the government house, events wouldn't have conspired to burn it down)—were the governor's mansion instead of a tourist spot? Would we be a city of skyscrapers, art museums and industries? Would our big city be soulless or a holder of bigger charms?

What if? It's a useless exercise in the grand scheme of things, I suppose, but a charming one to contemplate, nonetheless.

Suggested Reading

As stated previously, I in no way covered all of the events, or even all of the important ones in New Bern's history. I made allusion to a few major events but did not go into details—it wasn't possible with a book of this order. Perhaps I will write more thoroughly on individual subjects in the future. In the meantime, here are some other books that will help give you a better overall picture of New Bern's past:

Crown of Life, by Gertrude S. Carraway (1940). If there is any historian whose name will forever be associated with New Bern history, it is Ms. Carraway. Here is her history of Christ Church, but it covers a number of historical events outside the church as well.

The History of the First Presbyterian Church of New Bern, by Lachlan Cumming Vass and John Murphy Smith (1886). A kind of one-two punch, this is the reprint of a classic nineteenth-century history by Reverend Vass (1886) and a newer history catching up through 1987. Especially in Vass's work, you will experience a lot of colorful characters, stories and interesting photographs and illustrations.

A New Voyage to Carolina, by John Lawson (1967). I have a 2003 reprint of the 1960s edition edited by Hugh Talmage Lefler, and the book is practically falling apart from marginal scribbles and use. Written in 1709, it is Lawson's journal of his 1701 travels through the Carolinas and includes some of the best eyewitness information existing today on the lives of the Indians in the area, as well as observations on plant and animal life and the lives of European settlers.

Von Graffenried's Account of the Founding of New Bern, by Vincent H. Todd (1920). This is a reprint and commentary on Baron de Graffenried's account of New Bern's founding in French, German and English. It is the only source we have that tells us what happened at the start of the Tuscarora War, when De Graffenried and Lawson were held captive by the Tuscaroras in their town, Catechna (near present-day Grifton, North Carolina). Much of the book's purpose was to draw criticism away from himself for the town's early failures, and he spends a lot of time vilifying just about everyone else around him. It is a decidedly biased rendition of events, but it is still the only known rendition and provides a lot of interesting information and local color.

Governor Tryon and His Palace, by Alonzo Thomas Dill (1955). This is one of the better biographies of William Tryon's sojourn in North Carolina.

History of New Bern and Craven County, by Alan D. Watson (1987). Though it is dry, this is probably your best source for a full history of New Bern, from its founding to the latter part of the twentieth century.

The War of the Regulation and the Battle of Alamance, May 16, 1771, by William S. Powell (1975). This is a nifty little booklet (twenty-eight pages) that you can purchase cheaply at many historic sites or online.

James City: A Black Community in North Carolina 1863–1900, by Joe A. Mobley (1981). The story of how James City came about and grew up through the arrival of the Jim Crow years.

New Bern History 101, by Edward Barnes Ellis Jr. (2009). Here is an easy reading, informal introduction to many things New Bernian. Mr. Ellis touches on a number of events I have not and gives a good overview of many major events in New Bern's history. Unlike a lot of histories, he includes a fair amount of recent history.

Remembering Craven County: Tales of Tarheel History, by Bill Hand (2006, The History Press). It may sound immodest of me to suggest my own books, but this includes a selection of essays on local people and events that (for the obvious reasons of repetition) I did not cover in this volume.

A Walking Guide to North Carolina's Historic New Bern, by Bill Hand (2007). This book concentrates on the story behind a number of historic homes and churches, as well as the Cedar Grove Cemetery. It is written so that you can walk the historic district and read about what you're seeing as you go.

About the Author

Raised in Pennsylvania, Bill Hand has lived in the New Bern area since 1995. The fascinating past of this small town awakened his interest in history, and he has spent the years here digging into New Bern's past, as well as, over the past three years, sharing the events and personalities with the community through a weekly column in the *New Bern Sun-Journal*.

Bill also writes, directs and performs in plays through his theatrical company, Athens of the South Productions, and dabbles a bit in creative video as well. He graduated from Geneva College in Beaver Falls, Pennsylvania, in 1981 with a degree in literature and theater.

He lives just outside of New Bern with his wife, Roberta, and his daughter, Rachel. Another daughter, Sara, resides nearby.